Contents

Abbreviations

AIDS	Acquired Immune Deficiency Syndrome
CAP	Common Agricultural Policy
CFP	Common Fisheries Policy
COREPER	Committee of Permanent Representatives
COSAC	Conférence des Organes Spécialisés dans les Affaires Communautaires (Conference of Community and European Affairs Committees)
EBLUL	European Bureau for Lesser Used Languages
EC	European Community
ECHR	European Convention on Human Rights
ECJ	European Court of Justice
EFA	European Free Alliance
EP	European Parliament
EU	European Union
GDP	Gross Domestic Product
IGC	Inter-Governmental Conference
MEP	Member of the European Parliament
MP	Member of Parliament (Westminster)
NATO	North Atlantic Treaty Organisation
NCIS	National Criminal Intelligence Service
NGO	Non-Governmental Organisation
RTF	Radio Télévision Française
SNP	Scottish National Party
TEU	Treaty on European Union
UK	United Kingdom of Great Britain and Northern Ireland
USA	United States of America

Who's Afraid of a European Constitution?

Neil MacCormick

imprint-academic.com

Published in the UK by Imprint Academic
PO Box 200, Exeter EX5 5YX, UK

Published in the USA by Imprint Academic
Philosophy Documentation Center
PO Box 7147, Charlottesville, VA 22906-7147, USA

ISBN 1 84540 039 9

A CIP catalogue record for this book is available from the
British Library and US Library of Congress

*

Professor Sir Neil MacCormick is Leverhulme
Research Professor and Regius Professor of Public Law in the University of Edinburgh.

This book recasts for publication the Gregynog
Lectures for 2004 given in the University of Wales
at Aberystwyth in October 2004 under the title
'Europe: A Democratically Constituted Union?'

Prologue

I was born in 1941, into a highly political family, deeply engaged in the Scottish national movement that finally resulted in a re-established parliament in Scotland in 1999. I came to consciousness in the circumstances of war and its aftermath. Gradually becoming aware of a political world beyond Scotland, and then beyond the UK, I did not grow into even a vague and instinctive belief that peace, stability, and democracy would become dominant characteristics of continental Europe. To my childish eyes, there seemed an abundance of danger and instability.

From the vantage point of 2005, things look very different. Complacency in the face of declining electoral participation would be misplaced. Even so, democratic institutions and the habits of democratic life — free speech, mutual tolerance, jaw-jaw rather than war-war, settling issues by debates and votes — are deeply embedded in the way of life of northern, western, and southern Europe, and seem to be taking root successfully in middle and eastern Europe as well. Through the Council of Europe and the Court of Human Rights, respect for fundamental rights is everywhere substantial, and growing always more deep-rooted.

The countries of the European Union have played a particularly strong part in the consolidation of democracy and human rights. They have developed a single market (still by no means a perfect one) in which the decent prosperity of others becomes the key to one's own decent prosperity, not a threat to it. Ordinary Europeans in these countries are better off than their ancestors, and have experienced a longer period of internal peace than ever in their history heretofore. Enlargement of the Union offers the prospect of similar benefits to countries with less fortunate recent histories.

It would be false to claim that the existence of the European Union was the sole or perhaps even the dominant cause of all the benign developments of which I speak. NATO and the American involvement it guaranteed, mutual defence in the Cold War, the Council of Europe as distinct from the Community or the Union — all these and others belong prominently in any account of the transformation of Europe in the second half of the twentieth century. But no such account could fail to place the development of the European Communities — the Coal and Steel Community, the Economic Community, and Euratom — and then (since 1992) of the European Union as belonging among the vital elements of these changes. The European Union is far from faultless, but it has nevertheless been massively positive in its overall contribution to the lives of Europeans.

'If a thing ain't broke, don't fix it' is ancient wisdom. Anyway, ancient or not, it is a wise saying. This short book may seem to fly in its face. For it contains arguments in favour of adopting the currently proposed Constitution for the European Union (one which, perhaps too grandly, styles itself simply a 'Constitution for Europe'). I argue for fixing what seems to be an unbroken thing. I do so in a dual capacity — first as a philosopher of law and long-term student of problems in legal and political theory; secondly, as one who had the opportunity to participate in the Convention on the Future of Europe. To that Convention fell the task of seeing whether it would be possible to draft a sensible, workable, and acceptable constitution for the EU, replacing the current Treaties that define and empower the Union and its Institutions, but sustaining continuity with the mainly successful developments of the past half-century.

Truly, the thing ain't broke. But it is seriously flawed. Above all, it is not yet sufficiently democratic in its organisation. The 'democratic deficit' in the European Union is real, and really needs to be fixed. That is, to my judgement, what this proposed constitution is really for. The argument for this starts in Chapter 1.

Before then, I have several debts of gratitude to acknowledge. First is to Imprint Academic, the publishers *Societas*, and to Professor John Haldane for introducing me to them. I share their sense that it should be possible for serious ideas to be presented to a concerned public, drawing on the vast learning of philosophers and theorists in such domains as politics and law, yet presenting big ideas briefly,

and in plain and approachable terms. I hope this book will make a
contribution to this.

If it does, it will also be partly on account of the book's origins. In
October 2004, I was invited to present the 2005 Gregynog Lectures
in the University of Wales at Aberystwyth, under the title *Europe: A
Democratically Constituted Union*? and during the latter part of 2004
and early 2005, I have fulfilled invitations to lecture on connected
themes in my home University of Edinburgh, and in the University
of Cambridge, Strathclyde University, Birkbeck College and King's
College in London, and this has followed on visits during the Convention and its aftermath to universities and other fora in Bari, Flor-
ence, Warsaw, Inverness, Glasgow, Perth, with preparations also to
speak later in 2005 in Cornell, Texas, Sydney, Granada and Berlin.
All this has provided opportunities to clarify and improve the mes-
sage I am trying to impart, and to correct obvious errors — though
doubtless quite a few remain.

Political friends and colleagues in the Scottish National Party and
in the Group of the Greens and European Free Alliance in the European Parliament during 1999 to 2004 supported me and gave me the
opportunity to participate in the Convention, an extraordinary
opportunity for someone with my intellectual and academic interests and background.

I owe great debts to my own parliamentary assistants in that
period, Flora MacCormick, Craig Munro, Rina Moore, Elizabeth
Skinner and Sheena Cleland, who in particular helped in putting
together a political pamphlet *Europe: a Union of its Own Kind?* published with the support of the Greens/EFA Group in 2004, in which
some of the arguments presented here got a first airing.

Finally, in all my present work I have a vast debt to the
Leverhulme Trustees for the grant of a Personal Research Professor-
ship, held at the Law School of the University of Edinburgh for the
purposes of research on 'Law, State and Practical Reason'. I hope it
will be obvious that this book belongs in the relevant body of work.

Chapter 1

A democratic deficit

Do you know that you can be arrested in the United Kingdom on the basis of a warrant issued by a Danish or a Spanish or a Portuguese or a Belgian Court (among others)? This must be done through a request in English or accompanied by an English translation and sent to the National Criminal Intelligence Service (NCIS), or the Crown Office where the request concerns Scotland. Hitherto, full extradition requests have been made through diplomatic channels. This political oversight of extradition requests is abolished for European Arrest Warrant countries. The upshot will be that through a quick and simple process you can be sent to face interrogation and possible trial over there. The same can happen the other way round, of course. A person in Denmark or Portugal can be arrested on the basis of a warrant issued in the UK, and brought to trial here after only a brief appearance in a home court to check that all is in order.

Putting this more formally, since 1 January 2004, the United Kingdom has recognised and is operating the 'European Arrest Warrant' system. This has been achieved through Part I of the Extradition Act 2003. The system enables an arrest warrant issued in one member state of the European Union to be executed by a judicial order in another. This is subject to various safeguards. For example, there has to be proof of the identity of the individual before the executing court as the individual named in the warrant to be executed. Appropriate forms must be used, and use of the warrant is restricted to allegations about offences belonging to a statutory list of very serious offences. There are various negative conditions that block the use of the warrant, such as that there must be no ground for suspicion that the individual is being arrested for purposes of religious or racial persecution, or on account of sexual orientation or the like.

However, no part of the judicial process in the UK involves any qualitative assessment of the evidence prima facie available against the individual. There is a radical departure here from traditional extradition procedures (which remain in force in respect of non-EU countries). It is presumed that Courts or other competent legal authorities throughout the EU act in a fair, reasonable and responsible way in issuing warrants for arresting people suspected of serious crimes. One ground for this assumption is provided by Article 6 of the Treaty on European Union. Under it, all member states in the EU are required to observe the rule of law and fundamental human rights as recognised in the constitutional traditions of the Union's states and, more particularly, in the European Human Rights Convention. Each Member State ought therefore to assume unless the contrary is proven (by invocation of Article 7) that every other EU state conducts its criminal justice system in accordance with the same common minimum standards of respect for rights of persons suspected of criminal misconduct.

When what became Part I of the Extradition Act was being debated in the Westminster Parliament, many voices of concern were raised both in the Commons and the Lords, and some were raised in the press as well. Basic liberties, it was said, might be at risk because of oppressive foreign prosecutions without any real safeguards being available such as English habeas corpus or Scottish 'hundred and ten day' rule. Courts in the UK might be utilised as instruments to facilitate prosecutions – and detention for long periods pending prosecution – in criminal justice systems falling well short of the rigorous standards of justice observed here, it was said.

At least, however, one might think, the democratic will of the UK Parliament prevailed. What is done to enforce European Arrest Warrants is done by the will of and under legislation enacted by our own elected representatives. What could be more democratic than that? Anyway, if it does not work satisfactorily, those same representatives can in their own wise judgement revoke or amend it, can't they?

Well, no. They can't, nor could they in the first place amend the Government's Bill that became the 2003 Act. Why not? The answer is that the United Kingdom had an obligation under the Treaty on

European Union ('TEU' hereafter) to give effect to Council Framework Decision of 13 June 2002 'On the European arrest warrant and the surrender procedures between Member States' (2002/584/JHA). Framework Decisions of this kind are made under Article 39 of the TEU, and create a binding obligation on all member states to enact appropriate legislation according to their own constitutional arrangements in order to bring the framework decision into effect as law on the same terms throughout the Union. So actually Parliament could not amend the Bill, except perhaps if it had seen a way to bring it better in line with the Framework Decision. Nor can Parliament unilaterally repeal it either, except as part of a programme to renounce UK Membership of the EU, by repeal of the European Communities Act of 1972 and subsequent associated legislation including that ratifying the Maastricht Treaty.

Still, it could be said, the democratic will was really being served, because the Framework Decision was a decision by the Council of Ministers. Our elected government took its full part there, and did so following an agreement at the European Council ('the Tampere Summit') to act most speedily in favour of more effective mutual recognition of judicial decisions in criminal matters around Europe.

This was part of the programme to crack down on cross-border crime, people trafficking, drug trafficking, and all the rest of it. After '9/11' there has been a heightened awareness throughout Europe of the need for more effective co-operation against common threats. Moreover, it is a bit silly to have free movement of persons throughout the Union if there is not also effective cross-border law enforcement. On such grounds, not only did elected governments endorse and enact the Framework Decision, but the European Parliament was involved, too. So democratic controls were in place, and what was done addressed real and serious concerns of citizens in a remarkably expeditious way and with clear lines of responsibility.

Alas, this is at best half true. Things are improving somewhat, but at the time of the Framework Decision, all meetings of the Council of Ministers were held in private, indeed, in secret. Each would be preceded by even more impenetrable meetings of the Committee of Permanent Representatives (COREPER). This is not the 'Brussels bureaucracy', if by that you mean the European Commission and its civil service. But it is the national bureaucracies meeting in confidential conclave in Brussels to prepare the ground for their Ministers. In the upshot, anyway, it is almost impossible for the

Parliaments of the Member States to have, in advance of such a decision, any effective debating or decision-making process that secures effective answerability of their Ministers for the line they take on it. Nor can the European Parliament at present fill this gap effectively. For under Article 39 of the Treaty on European Union, Parliament is only consulted. Here, it does not have the power of co-decision as an equal legislative chamber alongside of the Council. It has that full legislative role in a whole lot of issues mainly affecting the 'common market', though not even all of it, for really sensitive matters like the Common Agriculture policy and the Common Fisheries policy are kept well clear of full co-decision. All the more so are Union matters involving defence and foreign affairs and those (like the arrest warrant) touching on Justice and Home Affairs.

Thus we can conclude that democratic controls are sadly lacking in matters which may go to the very heart of the basic liberties of human beings and citizens throughout the EU. The Arrest Warrant is a case in point. The idea is, let us concede, a perfectly reasonable one in itself. But it should never become law just on the say-so of Ministers set up for doing it by COREPER, insulated from parliamentary answerability either in their home parliaments or in the European Parliament. This is true even though the requirement to consult the European Parliament entails a thorough and public discussion of such a proposal, first in Committee and subsequently in Plenary Session, on receipt of a report prepared by the responsible committee. A rapporteur will have carefully worked over a draft report in dialogue with other members of the Committee interested in the issue, with Commission officials and perhaps even the responsible Commissioner in person, and with Council officials as well. In this procedure, Parliament is able to suggest amendments and improvements, and get a public airing for them (some of us proposed an amendment to build a kind of 'European habeas corpus' into the Arrest Warrant procedure. But this made no headway since it was considered too late to influence the final text and since it was known to be unacceptable to the Council.)

The Council is, however, under not the slightest obligation to pay any heed to what the Parliament says. Significantly, Parliament was assured at the time of giving its approval to the Report on the Arrest Warrant that it would at an early date be balanced by a measure allowing for 'Euro-bail'. This was a plan to facilitate conditional release of persons in pre-trial detention in a different member state from their own, on account of the availability of the Arrest Warrant to ensure non-default on the conditions of bail in such cases. No proposal has yet taken shape on this, and my understanding is that Commissioner Vitorino had to let the matter drop in the face of lack of Council support for the 'Euro-bail' idea, so to some extent Parliament may have bought into the Arrest Warrant proposal on a dodgy prospectus. All in all, the absence of full democratic accountability in such matters should be viewed with real concern.

This is the kind of concrete example that gives vivid content to the oft-mentioned 'democratic deficit' — there is a real, not just a theoretical, loss to citizens in the control their representatives can exert, even upon basic aspects of civil liberty.

If it were not possible to deal with this problem, we would have ground to be deeply concerned about the continuing acceptability of membership in the European Union. Those who attack it as undemocratic in its core would have real ammunition for their case. The good achieved by having the Union might really be outweighed by the damage that comes from undermining democracy — just as the cross-party 'SOS democracy' group in the European Convention and the European Parliament have contended.

Very well, then: can nothing be done? Yes, most certainly something can be done. There are three things in the currently proposed Constitution of the EU that will bring about exactly what seems to be needed. The first thing is to ensure that Member States' Parliaments are given better advance awareness of proposals that are before the Council, for then they will have better ability to check on their own ministers' activity at the Council. The second is to abolish the rule of secrecy concerning deliberations and votes in the Council when it is making laws, for then Ministers will also be better answerable after the event. The third is to ensure that the European Parliament is not left in the position of a mere consultee in the enactment of laws affecting fundamental liberties of all Europeans. The confederal character of the Union indeed justifies the legislative role of the States' governments in the Council of ministers and preparatory agencies like COREPER and its sub-committees. But to be democratic as well as confederal, the Union has to have two legislative chambers, and the second, the Parliament, is the one that represents citizens directly and in a broadly fair way through the principle of proportional representation.

These three democratic essentials are at the centre of the institutional scheme laid out in the Constitution (in Part I, which contains the real meat of the Constitution). To make matters yet clearer, the old terminology of 'directive', 'regulation', 'framework decision' is abandoned for referring to the Union's legislative instruments. These in fact take primacy over the laws of the member states, and have to be acknowledged as also being full-dress laws. Henceforward, there are to be 'European laws', that are binding in their entirety on all persons in the Union, and 'framework laws', that is 'legislative act[s] binding, as to the result to be achieved, upon each Member State to which it is addressed, but [leaving] to the national authorities the choice of form and methods.' In future, 'regulations' will solely be items of delegated rule-making, and decisions will also be binding, but only as addressed specifically to some person or persons, natural or juridical. (Article I-33).

The opportunity for advance warning of National Parliaments emerges from the strengthened principle of subsidiarity, and will be further discussed later. The rule about openness of all legislative deliberations in all law-making bodies is contained in Article I-54(2) 'The European Parliament shall meet in public, as shall the Council when considering and voting on a draft legislative act.'

Other important reinforcements of democratic accountability are to be found in the provisions concerning the election of the President of the European Commission by Parliament, and the continuing power of dismissal of the whole Commission, and, in effect, of individual Commissioners who neglect or abuse their office. We shall consider these and other reinforcements later.

Some may nevertheless say that we should reject the Constitution and thus get rid of the EU. They should beware. That would not actually be a good reason for rejecting the Constitution. Even those who actively wish to get rid of the EU, or get the UK out of it, need to reflect on the point that rejecting this Treaty/Constitution does not entail the abolition of the existing EU. What it does entail its continuance of the EU under the old Treaties as most recently amended by the Treaty of Nice. The undemocratic monstrosity of the legislative introduction of the European Arrest Warrant is one product of the legal structure established through these Treaties. Rejecting the Treaty/Constitution keeps the EU in being just as it is, but in worse shape than it need be. It also entails keeping an EU which has no express 'exit clause' to ease the path out of the Union for any state that does want to leave — perhaps the UK, if sceptics ultimately have their way.

The most fundamental case for endorsing and ratifying the Constitution is that it actually builds basic democratic requisites right into the foundations of the EU under a reformed constitutional order. It is the present Union that is on some points radically deficient, and urgently needing to be fixed.

Deliberately, and following ancient literary advice, I have started this book 'in the midst of things'. People concerned about the kind of problem I have just raised will, I hope, find it worthwhile to read the rest, in search of a more systematic account of the whole case for the Treaty, with an attempt to meet some of the well-known objections to it. The objections all deserve to be taken seriously. Each, however seems to me in the end unconvincing, as I hope my readers will also find them to be.

The more systematic account to follow deals with the following points, chapter by chapter, as detailed in the table of contents: How did the Draft Constitution Come about? What is in this Constitution? Does it Handle Human Rights satisfactorily? Is it too long and detailed? Do we want a Constitution at all? Will the EU become a Superstate if the Constitution is adopted? Is European-scale Democracy possible at all? Accountable Executives? What is 'Subsidiarity', and Why does it Matter? Do the 'Regions' get their proper place in Europe? Fisheries as a Special Problem.

Chapter 2

How did the Draft Constitution come about?

The Convention — who and what?

Following the Treaty of Nice, which paved the way for the remarkable and welcome enlargement of the European Union that occurred on 1 May 2004, with further instalments to come, the Union's leaders acknowledged the need for a wide-ranging consultation on its future shape. This would be aimed at re-connecting the Union with its increasingly alienated citizens. What came to be called the 'Constitutional Convention' (strictly, 'the Convention on the Future of Europe') was established by the Laeken Declaration of December 2001, following on the European Summit meeting. It was created with a remit to lead an open and far-reaching public debate on the future constitutional and institutional structures of the EU. The process involved parliamentarians as well as governments for the first time in relation to a full-scale revision of the Treaties prior to an Inter-Governmental Conference ('IGC'). It was modelled on the highly successful Convention that drafted the Charter of Fundamental Rights of the EU, adopted at Nice in December 2000, though only as a 'political declaration'.

Chaired by former French President Valéry Giscard d'Estaing with two Vice Presidents, former Belgian Prime Minister Jean Luc Dehaene, and former Italian Prime Minister, Giuliano Amato, the Convention began its work on 28 February 2002, and finished on 10 July 2003.

The Convention comprised

- governmental representatives of all Member States, acceding states and candidate states — twenty-eight in all, each with an alternate.

- representatives from the national parliaments of all Member States, acceding states and candidate states — fifty-six in all, each with an alternate.

- sixteen MEPs elected by the European Parliament on a party-proportional basis, each with an alternate, and two representatives from the European Commission, Michel Barnier and Antonio Vitorino.

- observers including the European Ombudsman, and representatives from the Economic and Social Committee and the Committee of the Regions.

- a Secretary-General, Sir John Kerr, former head of the UK Foreign Office, assisted by an extremely able and industrious secretariat drawn from the civil service of the Council, the Parliament, and the Commission.

Given the number of full and alternate members, at Convention sessions there could be up to two hundred and five persons in the room actively engaged in the debate, with a further thirteen observers entitled to speak. Then there were assistants, advisers to ministers, diplomats, press persons and Convention Staff. The remarkable thing was the extent to which Convention Members attended to their task and both contributed to the debates and listened to others' contributions as well. When the Convention was sitting there was always a considerable buzz in and around the large Committee Room (PHS 0C50) in the European Parliament building in Brussels, and in the adjacent public space and Hemicycle Bar. This may not be a perfect way to try to write a constitution, but it certainly had the merit of drawing the arguments out into open air and subjecting them to genuinely critical debate that led to modification of positions by all or most participants.

I speak of this from direct experience, for I was one of the alternate members representing the European Parliament at the Convention. As a Scottish National Party MEP for Scotland, I was a member of the 'European Free Alliance' (EFA), a group of like-minded parties representing various of the 'stateless nations' of Europe. Since 1999, the EFA has joined forces with the Green Party to form a Parliamentary Group, 'The Greens/EFA Group' in the European Parliament. In a closely contested election in our group, Austrian Green

Johannes Voggenhuber beat me by two votes in a third and final ballot for the position of Member of the Convention, so that I took up the position of alternate member.

Openness of deliberation was fostered by publication on the Convention website of all its official documents, all Contributions by Members, all Amendments proposed by them, and the verbatim record of proceedings.[1] This connected also to the Forum website, where citizens at large and non-governmental organisations (NGOs) could state and explain their opinions. It was disappointing that during a long period the print and broadcast media in Europe, and (as usual) particularly those of the United Kingdom, made but few comments and published few reports of what was going on. At the conclusion of the Convention's deliberations, newspapers in the UK, and some elsewhere, represented the output of the Convention as a sudden and unexpected bombshell that had been cooked up in some kind of secret conclave. This was very far from the truth. There has never been a more open and public process of constitution-drafting in the history of humankind.

How the Convention worked

The Convention's work was divided into phases. The first was that of 'listening', with wide-ranging consultations across Europe. Then came a phase of 'analysis', with a dozen working groups examining such major issues such as subsidiarity; the place of the Charter of Fundamental Rights in the EU Constitution; the EU's legal personality and how to simplify the Treaties; the role of national parliaments; defence and external affairs; and so on. Reports of the Working Groups were debated in plenary sittings of the Convention during the autumn of 2002 and through to early winter 2003.

Last was the 'writing phase'. Following on the publication and initial discussion of a Preliminary Draft, a framework document presented to the Convention in October 2002, there commenced in early winter of 2003 the serious job of fleshing out the skeleton table of constitutional contents with draft Articles. This was overseen by the Praesidium, which comprised the President and Vice-Presidents, two European parliamentarians, two national parliamentarians, two Commissioners, two national government representatives, and Mr Peterle from Slovenia to watch for the interests and concerns

---

[1]   Still available at http://european-convention.eu.int

of acceding states. Already the Convention was determined that these must be articles of a draft constitution, not just a revised treaty.

As each *tranche* of first draft articles was delivered, a torrent of amendments flowed in from the pens of the Members and Alternate Members of the Convention. In May and June, the Praesidium of the Convention responded to amendments and debates about the Articles by re-drafting and re-drafting again. The end-game in June and early July of 2003 was exceedingly hectic. The final text was hammered out by such consensus as could be achieved in each of the sub-sets of the whole Convention, and in the political groups that participated in it. The President presented the Convention's final conclusions comprising Parts I and II of the Draft Constitution-text to the governments of Member States at the European Council in Thessaloniki on 20 June 2003. On 18 July, after final adjustments concluded on 10 July, the text of Parts III and IV (the latter of which had received minimal discussion at the Convention) was delivered to Prime Minister Berlusconi in Rome at the beginning of his period as President-in-Office of the European Council.

In October 2003, the Inter-Governmental Conference assembled to discuss whether to adopt the Draft Constitution through an appropriate Constitutional Treaty, with or without amendment of the Convention's text. Member States each submitted points on which they requested or required further revision before they could sign a Treaty embodying the Constitution. After an abortive summit in Brussels in December 2003, the Irish Presidency made better progress during 2004, and set a course for conclusion of a Constitution-Treaty in June 2004. This was actually achieved at a Meeting on 17th and 18th June 2004 in Brussels, and the text as finally perfected in all official languages[2] was signed in Rome on 29 October 2004, under the title 'Treaty Establishing a Constitution for Europe'

After stating the bare formal facts of the Convention's existence, composition, and performance, it is incumbent on me to say a few words about the experience of participation in it. What was that like?

---

[2]   There are twenty one languages covering the twenty five states, viz, Czech, Danish, Dutch, English, Estonian, Finnish, French, German, Greek, Hungarian, Irish, Italian, Latvian, Lithuanian, Maltese, Polish, Portuguese, Slovak, Slovenian, Spanish and Swedish.

The character of the Convention

The point about the Convention was its essentially open, public and parliamentary, perhaps I should say 'parliamentarian', character. The predominant number of its members were representatives from parliaments at Member State or All-Union level, and were members of one or other parliament. But they had no direct electoral mandate from their electors, and the degree to which parliamentary delegations fairly reflected all shades of opinion in the States was a matter of conjecture.

A big question was to what extent the Presidium would run the Convention, to what extent the Convention would take on a life of its own. Would the democrats prevail over the bureaucrats? On the whole, democracy won, though not without a lot of sabre rattling from the back-benches. The President made more than a few bold, and occasionally contested, assertions about the consensus of the Convention as he perceived it, and undertook a series of private meetings with various Prime Ministers and Presidents, and committed himself to some controversial positions in public speeches here and there. In the end of the day, we had to produce a constitution that would be acceptable to the Member States. Since it was therefore important to draw citizens' attention to the momentous ideas that were taking shape, I was less outraged by Giscard's tactics than were some of my colleagues. Convention members and alternates (hereinafter, 'conventioneers') depended on our particular emissaries to the Praesidium (for the European Parliament, these were Iñigo Mendez de Vigo and Klaus Hänsch) to rectify any gross mis-ascription of consensus by the President. Thus, for example, was suppressed the President's pet brainchild, an annual 'Congress of Europe' comprising the European Parliament in session together with representatives of every national parliament.

Gisela Stuart MP was one of two representatives[3] of the UK Parliament at the Convention. She served on the Praesidium as a representative of the National Parliamentarians. The UK Members from the two parliaments and from the Government held regular forty-five minute meetings together with staff from the UK Permanent Representation immediately before each of the Plenary Sessions, and Gisela kindly briefed us about ongoing business in the

[3]   The other was David Heathcoat-Amory MP (Conservative) and the alternates to these two were Lord Tomlinson (Labour) and Lord MacLennan of Rogart (Liberal Democrat).

Praesidium. From herself and from other sources one learned a little of the hectic and sometimes chaotic conduct of business at the Praesidium, with documents arriving late in the day. The same certainly applied to non-Praesidium Members, but this was in a context in which, at great speed, documents were being prepared for discussion in many languages, usually starting with the French-language version. It came as something of a surprise and a disappointment when in December 2003, in a Fabian Society pamphlet, Gisela gave a very damaging account of the proceedings at the Praesidium, especially as it worked in the closing weeks of the Convention, when the final text of the Constitution was being hammered out (Stuart, 2003). It is a matter for regret that this was not stated much more openly at that very time when others might have supported a demand for a different way of proceeding.

However that may be, Members of the Convention did occasionally demand, and secure that we had, votes on significant issues concerning the conduct of the Convention, for example, on whether to demand a Working Group on 'Social Europe'. But the method of consensus prevailed over the method of voting. This was both right and inevitable, since we were not a parliament elected to our task, but what I called earlier a 'parliamentarian' assembly. Towards the end, as I mentioned, the process of settling points of controversy relied particularly on the emergence of acceptable common positions through the various fractions of the Convention. That is to say, among the political families represented, and among the different subsets of the Convention — national parliaments, the European Parliament, the governments and the Commission.

On this, however, Gisela Stuart's December 2003 pamphlet is highly critical. The consensus, she implies, was only agreement among an inner group who had the essential say. On one point, though, I would take leave to correct her. She correctly notes that the Constitution's text changed at a late moment on a significant point: 'The provision making it explicit that the President of the Commission could not hold the post of President of Council was removed in the last days. Valéry Giscard d'Estaing explained this as being an "unnecessary statement, as both jobs were so demanding, that one person simply could not combine them."'(Stuart, 2003). That may indeed have been Giscard's view, but it was not only the reason for the change.

At a late meeting of the European Parliament Delegation, visited by Jean-Luc Dehaene for the purpose of trying to establish where consensus lay, concern was being expressed about the potential difficulties of a two-headed Europe with a Commission President and a Council President potentially pulling in opposite directions. I intervened to point out that it was only necessary to delete the then current text's prohibition on the Council President holding another mandate at EU level. If that were done, it would become open to the Council, if it so chose, to elect the Commission President to its chair. Of course, since the post is elective, this will never come about unless the Council decides it would be better than retaining a double presidency. That would happen only if the separation of the posts had become or had proved to be seriously problematic. This intervention, visibly supported by most MEPs present, led or contributed to the necessary deletion's being made in the final draft, and indeed the final text. It is such an obvious point that probably quite few people separately thought of it, and for all I know put it forward for consideration at other similar fractional discussions in the closing stages of the Convention.

In other ways, there was certainly a lot of openness, and a lot of listening to whoever wanted to speak to us, both collectively and as individuals. Vice-President Dehaene was responsible for the organised consultation of 'European Civil Society', and a formidable two-day session took place on 24-25 June 2002, with a European Youth Convention sitting in Brussels 10-11 July and reporting to the full Convention on 12 July. The degree to which such gatherings are truly representative is, of course, always open to challenge, and sceptics like Danish MEP and Conventioneer Jens-Peter Bonde drew attention to the substantially Europhile character of most of the organisations that did take part. I had my own reasons to be somewhat unimpressed with the way the Youth Parliament was put together, which effectively overrode my right to nominate a representative from EFA.

Quite apart from that sort of mass consultation, I, like other Conventioneers, embarked on a vigorous programme of consultation within my own constituency of Scotland.[4] As a representative of the

---

[4]   Gisela Stuart writes that at the Convention 'MEPs spoke for the institution of the European Parliament, not for the people who elected them' (Stuart, 2003, p. 18). This is very far from the truth, though indeed the case any of us wanted to make for our constituents was strengthened to the extent that the

European Free Alliance, I consulted with sister parties in Galicia, Andalucia, Euskadi, Catalunya, Flanders, Poland, Friesland, Latvia, Savoie, Brittany, and Moravia. At home I held meetings and consultations all round Scotland, and I spent two splendid days with Plaid Cymru at Llandudno in Wales during September 2002. It was my great good fortune that I was able to participate at all in the Convention. My position as an Alternate Member in the European Parliament delegation depended on a close-run election in my Parliamentary Group, that of the Greens and European Free Alliance. In fact, alternate members were able to take a large part in the deliberations, partly by sensible co-ordination with full members (my principal was the Austrian Green MEP Johannes Voggenhuber) and partly by the good will of the Presidency and Secretariat. There were also procedural devices that helped — in particular the 'blue card' which facilitated a brief (one minute) debating intervention during plenary sessions and thus permitted almost instantaneous response to points made by other speakers.

My favourite personal example of this was when President Giscard introduced the debate on the first draft of the Articles declaring values and objectives of the Union. There was in the draft a call for recognition of Europe's 'cultural diversity'. Various members, myself included, lodged amendments adding the words 'and linguistic'. This was important, since hitherto the Commission has resisted attempts by Parliament to authorise financial support for regional and minority languages of the Union, since the Commission regards such support as lacking a legal base in the current Treaties. Adding 'and linguistic' would therefore fill a real gap in the law to the advantage of minority national and regional languages within the Union. In his introductory remarks, the President was very dismissive. 'Of course we do not want to encourage more and more languages in Europe,' said he. Up went my blue card, and when I was called a little while later, I pointed out, to applause, that we were not seeking to multiply languages but to get fair recognition of the existing languages and existing linguistic diversity of Europe. I think that may well have been a moment when a point was won.

European Parliament Delegation was aligned with it. But all my interventions at the Convention were based on what I considered an appropriate constitutional structure for Europe in the light of the proper and legitimate interests of Scotland (my constituency) and of the other stateless nations whose representatives as an EFA member I represented at the Convention.

Alternates could also take a full part in the Working Groups, as I did in that on the Charter of Rights and that on Simplifying the Instruments of the Union. There was a particularly useful role to be played in relation to the Charter, on which the UK Government was very reluctant to move beyond political acknowledgement of the Charter Rights, and devices had to be agreed with a view to assuaging doubts. In the Simplification Group, Giuliano Amato gave a brilliant lead and we settled for the proposal to abolish 'Regulations' and 'Directives', and to introduce in their place the idea of 'European laws' and 'European framework laws', as was discussed previously in Chapter 1. This then appropriately reserves use of the concept of 'regulation' for delegated acts of commission or other bodies, Parliament and (where appropriate) Council retaining a right of prior approval or subsequent recall over all such regulatory acts. Given the degree to which citizens currently find the work of the Union unintelligible, simplification is certainly called for. It remains to be seen whether enough has been achieved in this line.

Anyway, enough has been said to describe the work and the character of the Convention. It did succeed in producing a Draft Constitution, and that Draft, with amendment on a small number of important and contentious points, is the main substance of the Constitution adopted by the IGC for ratification by the states. Whatever else is to be said, one can fairly conclude that never has a European Treaty been drawn up by a process more open to the public, or more open to input from ordinary parliamentarians unencumbered by the special obligations of government office. On the other hand, Ministers from the governments of all the states were also there, also taking a full part, and everyone knew that there was no point in producing a final text that the governments would simply reject. The open character of debate in the Convention also seems to have had an effect on the subsequent conduct of the IGC. Governments' 'red line' issues were publicly declared, and the basis of negotiations during the IGC was publicly stated. So were interim conclusions, for example those from the 'Naples conclave' of foreign ministers of November 2003. This preceded the abortive IGC plenary session of December 2003, at which it proved impossible to reach final agreement satisfactory to all of Spain, Poland, France and Germany concerning the basis for qualified majority voting in the Council. It was a considerable achievement of Irish diplomacy and negotiating skill to bring of final agreement in June 2004.

Chapter 3

What is in this Constitution?

Some people may be puzzled whether we should be talking about 'a Treaty' or 'a Constitution' at this stage. The Treaty we are talking about is called the 'Treaty Establishing a Constitution for Europe'. So which is it — treaty or constitution? The answer is 'both', in the following sense: This is a Treaty in that it is a solemn agreement between the states that are parties to it, binding under international law, whereby they together establish a 'European Union' and confer certain powers on it. They thereby continue in a new form the currently existing European Union and European Community (which is, confusingly, one component part of the present 'Union'). But when we look at what the Treaty contains, we find that its content is a 'Constitution', that is, the basic rules that define the character and membership of the Union and its functions, and constitute and define the powers of the institutions created to exercise the Union's functions, and that set limits to these powers.

If the Treaty is ratified by all the states, the European Union in its new form will take over from the old European Union and European Community. It will work by reference to the Constitution for Europe that is contained in this Treaty. The constitution will be legally in force because all the member States are legally bound to each other to honour their Treaty. In the working life of the Union, when acts are done and decisions taken, their validity will be determined by the constitution that the Treaty contains. When the European Court of Justice interprets and applies this basic body of law, it will interpret it as the Union's Constitution, not simply as a text containing a treaty binding in international law.

The ratification debate is a debate about whether to ratify the Treaty. The arguments for and against ratifying it turn on the question whether or not it would be good for the Union to have a Constitution and, if so, whether this would be a good constitution to have. So first of all let us see what is in the Constitution, and then go on to these other debates.

The Constitution contained in the Treaty runs to four hundred and forty seven Articles in Four Parts, and these are backed up by a considerable stack of protocols and annexes dealing with special issues. (The first two protocols make important provision about the role of national Parliaments in the Union and about applying the principles of subsidiarity and proportionality. The remainder are aimed at securing legal continuity with the past, including taking due account of the various agreements that were made on each occasion when new states came into the Union.)

Four hundred and forty seven Articles, drafted with legal precision, add up to a huge Treaty text. Few citizens will ever read any of them, even fewer will read all of them. How then can they possibly take an informed view about the Constitution?

My answer is that people should take the trouble to read Part I, just the first sixty Articles. If you are interested in the Constitution, that is the real heart of the matter, the core constitution itself. Read also, if you can, the Charter of Rights which makes up Part II of the Constitution. Like the Bill of Rights in the USA, the Charter of Fundamental Rights of the European Union is an essential counterpart to the powers the constitution gives to the European institutions. For it sets limits to these powers in favour of the citizens, indeed in favour of all persons in the Union. The Charter is highly readable, and runs only to a further fifty-four articles. The twelve Articles of part IV are also important. For they deal with how the Constitution is to come into force (if it is ratified), how to secure smooth succession and legal continuity between the existing legal and institutional framework and the new legal order laid down in the Constitution. They deal also with the territorial bounds in which the constitution will take effect (if at all), and how it is to be amended in the future. These are matters that obviously have to be regulated, but they do not need to be studied in detail or at all by ordinary citizens wanting to find out what the constitution is about.

The huge bulk of the Constitution is in Part III, comprising three hundred and twenty-two articles about 'the policies and functioning of the union'. The good news is that nobody needs to read all of these in order to understand the Constitution, for they do not strictly belong inside the core constitution properly so called. They are an essential adjunct to, but not an intrinsic part of, the core constitution of the Union as it will emerge if the Treaty is ratified. I will shortly explain why this is so, but let us start with a quick check on Parts I and II, which I claim to be the core of the thing.

Part I starts by establishing the Union, as one upon which, by will of the states and the citizens, the states confer certain powers. It then declares what are the values of the Union — human dignity, liberty, democracy, equality under the rule of law and respect for human rights, in a context of pluralism, tolerance, justice, solidarity and non-discrimination. It declares as Union objectives the pursuit of peace and the upholding of these values, and gives more detail about pursuing these values, along with respect for social cohesion and justice, sustainability, cultural and linguistic diversity and international distributive justice in a single market which is also an area of freedom security and justice. It re-asserts the four freedoms — free movement of persons, goods, services, and capital throughout the Union — and the ban on nationality-based discrimination. It commits the union to respecting the national identities of the Member States and the Member States to loyally co-operating in upholding the constitution and fulfilling the tasks it lays down for them. This will include acknowledging the continuing force of the primacy of the Constitution and laws made under it over the domestic law of each member state. It endows the Union with legal personality, and appropriate symbols — the flag, a motto, an anthem, a currency (the euro), and 'Europe day' as a day of common celebration (9 May).

Next, it formally adopts the Charter of Rights as laid out in part II, acknowledges the continuing obligatory character of the European Human Rights Convention and the constitutional traditions of the member States as the source of binding principles for the Union. It requires the Union to accede to the European Convention. And it restates the citizenship of the Union as belonging to all who have citizenship of any Member State, Union citizenship being additional to national citizenship, not a substitute for it.

Then we come to the central question: what is the Union competent to do? Title III of Part 1 states the three basic principles. The principle of conferral limits the Union to acting only on compe-

tences conferred by or under the Constitution. That of subsidiarity,
directs that the Union is to act only if and insofar as the objectives of
the proposed action cannot be sufficiently achieved by the Member
States, either at central level or at regional and local level. That of
proportionality prescribes that the content and form of Union
action shall not exceed what is necessary to achieve the objectives of
the Constitution. The competences themselves are next summa-
rised, in three groups — the exclusive competences of the Union,[1]
on which it alone can legislate; the shared competences,[2] concerning
which member States retain legislative power except to whatever
extent the Union has exercised its, and other competences that do
not involve Union legislation. These concern the provision of
arrangements to enable co-ordination of economic and employ-
ment policies of the Member States; the defining and implementing
of a common foreign and security policy; and areas in which the
Union can take supporting, co-ordinating or complementary action
in matters that remain essentially within the legislative and executive competence of the Member States.[3] A 'flexibility clause' creates
a procedure whereby the Council of Ministers can, with the consent
of the European Parliament and with due notice to National Parliaments, unanimously decide to take measures necessary to achieve
one of the Union's objectives for which the necessary powers are
missing in the Constitution.

It lies in the hands of the institutions of the Union defined in Title
IV of part I to exercise these competences. The Institutions are the
European Parliament, the European Council (comprising the Heads
of State and Government of the Member States); the Council of Ministers (one minister per Member State, normally voting by 'qualified

---

[1]   The relevant domains are: (a) customs union; (b) the establishing of the
      competition rules necessary for the functioning of the internal market (c)
      monetary policy for the Member States whose currency is the euro; (d) the
      conservation of marine biological resources under the common fisheries
      policy; (e) common commercial policy.

[2]   The relevant domains are: (a) internal market; (b) social policy, for the
      aspects defined in Part III; (c) economic, social and territorial cohesion; (d)
      agriculture and fisheries, excluding the conservation of marine biological
      resources; (e) environment; (f) consumer protection; (g) transport; (h)
      trans-European networks; (i) energy; (j) area of freedom, security and
      justice; (k) common safety concerns in public health matters, for the aspects
      defined in Part III.

[3]   The relevant domains are: (a) protection and improvement of human
      health; (b) industry; (c) culture; (d) tourism; (e) education, youth, sport and
      vocational training; (f) civil protection; (g) administrative cooperation.

majority'), the European Commission, and the Court of Justice. Additional institutions are the European Central Bank, managing the euro, and the Court of Auditors, checking the financial regularity of the Union's actions. There are two advisory bodies, the Economic and Social Council, representing 'the social partners' including employers' organizations and trade unions, and the Committee of the Regions, representing regional and local government within the Member States. The Parliament and the Council of Ministers act together in the exercise of legislative and budgetary powers, normally on the basis of initiatives taken by the Commission, which is also particularly answerable to (and dismissible by) the Parliament. Under a President (to be elected by the Parliament on the nomination of the European Council), the Commission will initially comprise one Commissioner from each Member State. Subsequently the number will only be two thirds of the numbers of member States (e.g., eighteen Commisssioners when there are twenty seven states). From that point on, there will be rotation of membership around the member states, on a principle of equality. The new President and the Council will 'by common accord' agree a list of nominee Commissioners, and the whole Commission will be subject to a 'vote of consent' by the European Parliament. Any member of the Commission must resign if requested to do so by the President, who otherwise has extensive powers to oversee the organization and working of the Commission.

The European Council has no legislative powers, but brings European leaders together to give impetus for developing the Union and by way of defining its general political directions and priorities. It is to have a President (who may not hold any national office) elected for two and a half years renewable, to co-ordinate and drive forward its activities and those of the Council (of Ministers). He/she will represent the Union externally, along with a new Union Minister for Foreign Affairs, also appointed by the European Council, who will be a Vice-President of the Commission in addition to her/his other duties. Much more will be said later in this book about the details of the formation and interaction of the institutions, in connection with further inquiry into the true character of the Union under this constitution, and its capacity to claw back the democratic deficit.

Concerning the exercise of Union competences, there are provisions already noted in passing concerning the different sorts of acts the Institutions can deploy. These are: legislative acts (laws and framework laws), subordinate rule-making (regulations), and non-legislative acts (decisions, with binding force on those to whom they are addressed, and recommendations and opinions, which do not have binding force). Rules about publication and entry into force of all such acts are appropriately provided for. Specific provisions are made for implementing policies on common foreign and security policy and common security and defence policy as well as policy on justice and home affairs (all of which used to be in separate 'pillars' of the Union as hitherto established by the Maastricht Treaty and its successors.) Provision is made to enable 'enhanced co-operation' among a subset (or subsets) of member States in relation to the exercise of non-exclusive competences of the Union — such enhanced co-operation may be serviced by the Union's general Institutions.

Provisions on the Democratic Life of the Union underline the point I already made about the required public character of all legislative acts. They also affirm the democratic equality of the citizens of the Union, and their rights to be represented through democratic institutions and to participate in its democracy both through dialogue with the institutions and by virtue of a right to take legislative initiatives. This will be by way of petitions of at least a million signatures inviting the Commission to take or initiate some appropriate Union action. Proceedings of all the Union's Institutions are subject to the maximum transparency with public rights of access to documents, but also with protection of data concerning individuals. The European Ombudsman is appointed by the European Parliament and is responsible for responding to and investigating complaints about irregularities in the acts of any of the institutions. Dialogue with the social partners has to be maintained, and also with churches and religious associations or communities, as well as 'philosophical and non-confessional organisations'.

Four Articles (supplemented with important clarifications and expansions in Part III) lay down budgetary and Financial principles, and other provisions on the Union's resources and the multiannual financial framework (both of which are determined by the Council subject to the assent of the parliament). The annual budget has to be enshrined in a European law passed by both the Council and the Parliament. At present, under law in force, the most that may be provided by way of annual expenditure in the multiannual financial framework is 1.28% of the gross domestic product of the Union. Current political pressures are towards reducing rather than extending this percentage. (By comparison, federal governmental expenditures in the USA run regularly at around 20% of GDP).

Article I-57 charges the Union with the task of maintaining good and co-operative arrangements with its neighbouring countries. Finally, the last three (58 — 60) Articles of Part I regulate membership of the Union, opening membership to all European States desirous of it, provided they uphold the Union's values, respecting the rule of law and human rights. If any Member State falls into serious and persistent breach of the values, suspension provisions may ultimately be brought to bear on it as determined by Council and Parliament (minus the suspect State's representatives) acting by special majorities. Last of all, it is provided that each state has the right to withdraw from the Union. It may do so by decision taken in accordance with its own constitutional requirements, on the basis that there should be a two-year period in which to determine a new relationship between the departing state and the continuing Union, if any can be agreed.

Even through such a rather breathless summary of its provisions as this one, it ought to be clear that Part I of the Constitution does state in pretty plain terms what the Union is for, what it is to be empowered to do and how it must do it, and through which agencies it can act, subject to what mutual checks and balances among themselves. Having often wrestled with the present jumble of treaties, even in their post-Nice consolidated form, I must say that Part I of the proposed Constitution is far more readily intelligible and reader-friendly that that which it will replace if it is ratified.

Then Part II, the Charter of Rights itself, dedicates a further fifty-four clearly presented Articles to laying down the fundamental rights persons[4] in the Union are to enjoy as against acts by the Union and its institutions. These bind the Member States only so far as they are engaged in implementing Union law (otherwise, their own constitutional arrangements specify the rights citizens and strangers have against the state, though all must live up to the standards set in the European Convention for the Protection of Human Rights and Fundamental Freedoms). The Charter rights run parallel to those in the European Convention and some more recent human

---

[4]   Very few of the rights in the Charter, e.g., those concerning voting in local elections and all-Union elections are reserved to Union citizens.

rights instruments. They are ranged under the rubrics of Dignity, Freedoms, Equality, Solidarity, Citizens' Rights, and Justice, followed by four 'horizontal articles' regulating the interpretation and range of application of the rights under the six main rubrics. The Charter is already in force as a 'political declaration' since the Treaty of Nice (2000), and it surely makes sense to incorporate it with legally binding effect in the Constitution, if a Constitution is to be adopted at all.

The starting point for this Charter that comprises Part II was in June 1999 at the European Council, meeting in Köln. It was decided to establish a 'Convention' of parliamentarians and governmental representatives to prepare a document declaring the rights citizens of the European Union enjoy in virtue of that citizenship. Citizenship of the Union had itself first been established by the Maastricht Treaty of 1991, but had been perceived as very much a damp squib. For little that was new came with it beyond the right of a citizen living in a member state other than her/his own to vote and stand for office in regional or local authority elections, and elections to the European Parliament. The Council hoped that some kind of solemn reminder of the panoply of rights associated with EU citizenship would help to re-connect citizens to the Institutions of Community and Union.

The Convention was chaired by Roman Herzog, former President of the German Federal Republic, and of its Constitutional Court. It was made up of sixteen representatives from the European Parliament, two members from each of the Parliaments of the fifteen Member States (thirty in all), a personal representative of the Head of State or Government of each member State, and a Member of the European Commission. Each full member had the backing of an alternate member, so the whole number of those participating was one hundred and eleven in all, along with various observers entitled to speak but not vote. The Convention started its work in December 1999. The 'Charter of Fundamental rights of the European Union' that it produced was received and approved by the European Council in Biarritz in October 2000. Eventually, in the Treaty of Nice, the Charter was recognised as a 'politically binding' instrument, but not as a legally binding part of the constitutional framework of the EU. The refusal to give it legally binding character was chiefly due to the UK government's obstinate resistance to this, for reasons that re-emerged in the later constitutional convention, of which I will say something in due course.

Scarcely was the ink dry on the signatures of the Treaty of Nice than the new process we have considered in Chapter two began to warm up. By the end of 2001, under the Belgian Presidency, the European Council meeting at Laeken resolved to call into being a fresh Convention, 'a Convention on the Future of Europe'.

Anyway, one can say that the core Constitution runs to sixty main articles, with a Charter of Rights that adds a further fifty-four. Another handful of articles in Part IV regulates the coming into force of the Constitution and the procedures for its future amendment and related matters. This is neither too long nor an enemy of intelligibility.

Chapter 4

Does it handle human rights satisfactorily?

Many people would agree, I suppose, with the idea that governmental power, especially at the all-Europe level must be limited power. Humans have fundamental rights, and institutions of government erected among us to serve the common good should never be able to cancel or ride roughshod over the fundamental rights of individual people. What could be plainer? The devil, as usual, lies in the detail. Once you start trying to define the rights in question, you may state them too broadly, or too vaguely, so that they either catch far too much or have to be worked out in more concrete terms by courts comprising judges from many different legal and judicial traditions. Surprising and unwelcome interpretations may emerge from this process, taking a form that is much harder to amend by democratic decision than it was to adopt the rights-text in the first place. Let us take an example.

In the Charter of Rights (Part II of the Constitution) Article II Article II-77, on the right to property, runs as follows:

> 1. Everyone has the right to own, use, dispose of and bequeath his or her lawfully acquired possessions. No one may be deprived of his or her possessions, except in the public interest and in the cases and under the conditions provided for by law, subject to fair compensation being paid in good time for their loss. The use of property may be regulated by law insofar as is necessary for the general interest.

> 2. Intellectual property shall be protected.

Intellectual property, we note, is to be protected — but which property in what kinds of 'thing'? For example, is computer software to be subject to protection by patents, or only by copyright as is the case at present? This is a highly controversial point in current legis-

lative debate. Certainly, any régime of intellectual property that is
adopted must secure adequate protection for the rights involved.
Once a decision is made, however, about patents for software (for
example) how revocable will it be? Could the legislature at a future
date revoke by ordinary legislative process laws earlier adopted by
that process extending patent protection under European Union
law in this debated case? Would that be an instance of a 'use of
property regulated by law in so far as is necessary for the general
interest'? Or would it amount to an unlawful removal of protection
from a species of intellectual property?

How far, again could legislation be adopted to prevent what
many people see as abuses of intellectual property rights, where
these work as obstacles to provision of generic drugs in poor countries afflicted with (e.g.) the AIDS epidemic? How do we hold in balance the right to life and health and the right to property?

Such questions are, doubtless, meat and drink to human rights
lawyers and to intellectual property specialists. They are also of
very general public and professional concern, as can be seen by
reference to the vigorous lobbying of MEPs that takes place on all
questions concerning intellectual property rights. Antinomies, difficulties, and balancing problems of such a kind explain the anxiety
some governments expressed during both the Charter Convention
and the Constitutional Convention about the prospect of adopting
the Charter as a legally binding instrument or, *a fortiori*, as a built-in
Part of a new 'Constitution for Europe'. The Charter is an attractive
document because it is written in simple and categorical terms,
without endless exceptions and qualifications being expressed. The
stylistic contrast with the 1950 Convention is striking — as an example in the endnote to this chapter perhaps makes vivid.

Difficulties, however, will inevitably arise from the existence of
two instruments, both about fundamental rights, binding on the
same persons and institutions. All the more will this be so when the
Constitution comes into force (if it does). For then the Union, having
acquired international legal personality, will itself have to accede to
the Human Rights Convention as foreseen in Article I-9 (2).

Citizens of the Union will confront institutions that are bound by
their own Constitution to respect the Charter in favour of all persons within the Union, while at the same time being bound as a matter of public international law to respect the European Convention
for the protection of Human Rights and Fundamental Freedoms.

Over the former, jurisdiction will belong to the European Court of Justice, over the latter, to the Human Rights Court in Strasbourg. Will there arise two varieties of fundamental rights jurisprudence, a Luxembourg interpretation of the rights and a Strasbourg interpretation of them? If so, which is to prevail in case of conflict? And how will all this dovetail with decisions of states' constitutional courts or other highest jurisdictions concerning human rights enshrined in domestic constitutions, or human rights binding through the 'domestication' of ECHR rights as achieved, e.g., by the (UK) Human Rights Act 1998? The better view, and the one more likely to prevail, is that the European Court of Human Rights at Strasbourg will be recognised as the absolute and final long-stop authority on human rights issues. All other jurisdictions should, and probably will, fall into line with its holdings, including those allowing a margin of national (or Union-wide) appreciation, especially concerning the concept of 'more extensive' protection. Thus may be avoided an indigestible superabundance of rights differently specified in different instruments, all of them legally binding.

Related to this problem is one concerning over-empowerment of judges. The UK Government in particular has a great horror of the idea that judges, especially judges in supranational tribunals, may conduct themselves after the fashion of unruly horses, running wild in the leeways of discretion afforded by vaguely-written instruments such as the Charter of Rights. How are the clauses on bodily integrity going to be read? What is the juridical cash-value of a right to strike — even one qualified as being 'in accordance with Union law and national laws and practices' — how strong a qualification is that in relation to the 'right to negotiate and conclude collective agreements at the appropriate levels and, in cases of conflicts of interest, to take collective action to defend their interests, including strike action' (see Article II-88)?

Commissioner Antonio Vitorino chaired a Working Group on the Charter of Rights and its incorporation in a constitution. Baroness Scotland, the UK government's alternate member at the Convention, argued there the case for those governments and others concerned about such issues. She pressed hard for recognition of the problematic character of the legal incorporation of Charter rights along side of rights under the European Convention for the protection of Human Rights and Fundamental Freedoms and rights derived from national constitutions and constitutional traditions.

The compromise eventually achieved was to strengthen the 'horizontal clauses' now enshrined in Articles II–111 to 114 to ensure that limitations on Union competences elsewhere in the constitution also limit the scope of applicability of the Charter rights. They also ensure that the constitutional traditions of the Member States shall have to be taken into account in interpreting the rights based on them. Also, the Articles of the Charter that express principles become judicially cognisable only to the extent that these principles may have been put into effect by legislative acts or executive decisions, and then only for the purposes of interpreting the Act or decision in question.

A further requirement set by the UK before it would agree to incorporating the Charter was aimed at ensuring that certain preparatory documents ('*travaux préparatoires*') should be available for judicial use as a guide to interpretation of the Charter if it came legally into force. These were 'the explanations prepared under the authority of the Praesidium of the Convention which drafted the Charter and updated under the responsibility of the Praesidium of the European Convention'. These are explicitly adopted into the final text of Article112, section 7: 'The explanations drawn up as a way of providing guidance in the interpretation of the Charter of Fundamental Rights shall be given due regard by the courts of the Union and of the Member States.'

As a participant in that Working Group, I strongly supported the incorporation of the Charter in the Constitution, but also tried to assist in overcoming apprehensions and objections such as those raised by Baroness Scotland. It would be unthinkable to have a new constitution but to say nothing about rights in it, and barely thinkable to shunt the rights into a siding labelled 'Political Declaration'. On balance, a reasonable compromise was achieved. The text with its 'explanations', and with the 'horizontal clauses' in the form they now take is well calculated to rein in any unruly horses that turn up in the Courts of the Union. Anything in the way of a legal instrument can turn out badly if it is interpreted and applied without regard to the need for overall coherence in the law and for a reasonable fit between interpretations in use in different tribunals whose authority extends over largely the same set of persons. There is no good reason to fear that in the European Courts over the long run judges will fail to take seriously these obligations in favour of coherent law.

Endnote: Human Rights Convention and Part II of the Constitution

It is instructive to compare Article II — 66 of the Charter with its ancestor, Article 5 of the 1950 Human Rights convention. The former is lapidary in its simplicity:

Article II-66

Right to liberty and security

Everyone has the right to liberty and security of person.

With this should be compared the relative verbosity, but also greater legal exactitude of:

Article 5

1. Everyone has the right to liberty and security of person. No one shall be deprived of his liberty save in the following cases and in accordance with a procedure prescribed by law:

(a) the lawful detention of a person after conviction by a competent court;

(b) the lawful arrest or detention of a person for non-compliance with the lawful order of a court or in order to secure the fulfilment of any obligation prescribed by law;

(c) the lawful arrest or detention of a person effected for the purpose of bringing him before the competent legal authority on reasonable suspicion of having committed an offence or when it is reasonably considered necessary to prevent his committing an offence or fleeing after having done so;

(d) the detention of a minor by lawful order for the purpose of educational supervision or his lawful detention for the purpose of bringing him before the competent legal authority;

(e) the lawful detention of persons for the prevention of the spreading of infectious diseases, of persons of unsound mind, alcoholics or drug addicts or vagrants;

(f) the lawful arrest or detention of a person to prevent his effecting an unauthorised entry into the country or of a person against whom action is being taken with a view to deportation or extradition.

2. Everyone who is arrested shall be informed promptly, in a language which he understands, of the reasons for his arrest and of any charge against him.

3. Everyone arrested or detained in accordance with the provisions of paragraph 1.c of this article shall be brought promptly before a judge or other officer authorised by law to exercise judicial power and shall be entitled to trial within a reasonable time or to release

pending trial. Release may be conditioned by guarantees to appear for trial.

4. Everyone who is deprived of his liberty by arrest or detention shall be entitled to take proceedings by which the lawfulness of his detention shall be decided speedily by a court and his release ordered if the detention is not lawful.

5. Everyone who has been the victim of arrest or detention in contravention of the provisions of this article shall have an enforceable right to compensation.

It is an interesting question how exactly the terms of the 'horizontal clause that is now Article II-112 (3) will reflect on the relationship between the longer text of 1950 and the shorter one of 2000/2004. It says:

Insofar as this Charter contains rights which correspond to rights guaranteed by the Convention for the Protection of Human Rights and Fundamental Freedoms, the meaning and scope of those rights shall be the same as those laid down by the said Convention. This provision shall not prevent Union law providing more extensive protection.

In itself, this pretty obviously means that all the exceptions and qualifications made explicit in ECHR Article 5 are impliedly present in Article II-66. The permitted 'more extensive protection' would have to be derived from a Union law other than the Charter itself, for if the Charter were read as itself extending protection, it would be utterly indeterminate as to how it does this. It seems more reasonable to consider that the Charter does not itself extend protection beyond that of the ECHR in those articles that deal with the same rights as the ECHR covers, but it does so in articles that cover new ground derived from other instruments subsequent to the ECHR. Otherwise it would be a matter for fresh lawmaking to provide more extensive rights, in a way that would not fetter or cramp other rights guaranteed in the Charter.

These suggestions are amply confirmed when one goes to the 'Declarations' annexed to the Constitution Treaty, in particular to the one that incorporates the '*travaux préparatoires*' that the judges must take into account. In respect of the right to liberty these say:

The rights in Article 6 (1) are the rights guaranteed by Article 5 of the ECHR, and in accordance with Article 52(3) of the Charter (2), they have the same meaning and scope. Consequently, the limitations which may legitimately be imposed on them may not exceed those permitted by the ECHR, in the wording of Article 5.

This is yet a firmer curb to set upon any unruly horse. Rights, surely, ought to be acknowledged in constitutions, and this text should not generate confusion.

Chapter 5

Is the Constitution too long and detailed?

The argument so far has established, I hope, that the core constitution, contained in Part I is by no means too long or obscure in its sixty articles. Part II adds an essential protection of fundamental rights, and does so in fifty four articles of exemplary clarity, with, however, a need to read them in tandem with the European Human Rights Convention. Reasonable people will not, I suppose, take too much exception to that. Many, however, reserve their wrath for the vast scope of Part III. Yet the Treaty that is before us for ratification contains this as an integral part of the Constitution it embodies.

Why is Part III there, and why so long? The answer is that Part III is there to preserve with appropriate amendments all the provisions of the present Treaties that have not been superseded by Part I. It amends these so as to make them conform with the constitutional framework declared in Part I. Thus it restates in the inherited terms all the provisions about the 'Policies and Functioning of the Union', with allowance for the new concept of Union laws and framework laws, and the new normal legislative procedure. It also restates certain basic principles common to all parts of the policies and functioning in a way that ensures Parts I and II do not by inadvertence seem to derogate from existing standards and requirements.

In relation to Common Foreign and Security Policy, Common Defence and Security Policy, Justice and Home Affairs, and Budgets, Part III also makes necessary supplements to the framework provisions in Part I. In relation to the Institutions, particularly the

Court of Justice, provisions on its jurisdiction and on access to it are again included in part III. Undeniably, elements like these in Part III do appertain to the core constitution, which carefully makes cross-reference to them. They do not, however, function at a level that needs study by the ordinary citizen concerned about the broad meaning of this scheme of government.

Moreover, most of Part III does not in the same way appertain to the core constitution at all. Mainly, this Part is an adjunct to the core constitution. The job it does is essentially to spell out exactly how each specific competence of the Union is to be understood and is to be exercised. Doing this job adds to the overall bulk, and it is perhaps regrettable for the sake of the ratification debates that Part III is built into the Constitution as such. It might preferably have been enacted at the same time by way of a body of associated fundamental law, with a somewhat lighter amendment procedure than applies to the Constitution in the strict and proper sense[1].

There can be no doubt, however, of the necessity to have done by some means the job that Part III does, and to have done it as part of the overall scheme of constitutional reform in the EU. This, after all, is to be a Constitution for a going enterprise, one which is intended to secure continuity of the whole ongoing body of law and practice that has been developed inside the European Community — the so-called *acquis communautaire*. To have left it for judicial and scholarly interpretation to figure out what part of the present treaties was repealed by the Constitution and how the unrepealed parts were to work in the context of a new framework Constitution would have been a citizens' nightmare. It would also have been a dripping roast for lawyers, with many years of needless legal uncertainty stretching ahead. The method of presentation of the material of Part III as integral to the very Constitution is open to question. The task achieved was, however, an absolutely vital one.

Above all, the performance of this task should be most welcomed by those who most fear 'competence creep', whereby the law-making institutions, with after-the-event approval from the Court, effectively extend the range of what they can do. The implication of

---

[1]   Indeed, Article IV-445 does establish a procedure whereby the bits of Part III that regulate the single market can be amended by a simplified procedure whenever the effect is to diminish competences exercised by the Union. This will call for a unanimous vote in the European Council followed by approval by the European Parliament and confirmation by each member state according to its own constitutional requirements.

the adoption of Part III is that nothing is changed except what is expressly changed. The real purpose of Part III is not for it to be read through at a single sitting, but to be referred to in respect of particular issues of moment-by-moment interest.

All in all, making full allowance for the great bulk of Part III, one may conclude that the Constitution states with a new clarity the union's real character. It is — rather, it is to be — a Union formed by joint decision of its member states, and it exercises only the powers that they confer on it. See Article I-1 and Article I-11. It is and remains for all its participants a voluntary Union. For the first time, it is explicitly stated, in Article 60, that any Member State may choose, by its own constitutional processes, to withdraw from the Union. The core constitution is by no means too long, or difficult to read and assimilate. The regrettably bulky Part III is there for a reasonable and proper purpose, but should not be put at the centre of arguments about the Constitution. Since it re-states in a rather more logical way what is already in existing Treaties, adjusting this to the core constitution, there is no particular point in voting against the Constitution as a protest against the bulkiness of part III. If the Constitution is rejected, the whole substance of Part III will still be in force. But it will remain less logically laid out, and encapsulated in a framework that is both harder to understand and less democratic than are the core provisions of this Constitution.

The work done in preparing Part III exhibits the importance of continuity and evolution in this process of constitution-making. The Constitution Treaty contains in its preamble words that the Convention did not include in its Draft, which amounted to a serious omission from it. These are as follow:

> DETERMINED to continue the work accomplished within the framework of the Treaties establishing the European Communities and the Treaty on European Union, by ensuring the continuity of the Community *acquis* …

This point is rammed home, and given copper-bottomed legal effect in Article IV-438, entitled 'Succession and legal Continuity' It is an absolutely vital point. The Constitution does not invent the Union out of nothing. It reconstitutes a going concern, which already has a kind of 'functional constitution', as will be argued in the following chapter. Immodestly, I must say I moved a partly unsuccessful amendment in the Convention to make a similar point, but with only partial success at the time. The always present paradox of constitution making is that only those who are already constituted in some kind of a polity can adopt a constitution, but persons only become members of a polity by having that character bestowed upon them by a constitution. A Constitution makes you a citizen, but you have to be one to adopt a constitution. The dialectic of *pouvoir constituant* and *pouvoir constitué* is indeed puzzling, until one reflects on the always-present element of custom and tradition in real-life constitutional processes.

If the European Coal and Steel Community and the European Economic Community and Euratom had never existed nothing that is happening now would have happened in just this way. But these organisations, with an interestingly novel institutional structure including one 'Court of Justice of the European Communities', were set up five decades ago by Treaties among the original six (Belgium, France, Germany, Italy, the Netherlands, and Luxembourg). In due course, the Court decided that the EC Treaty in particular, by necessary implication, had to be interpreted as binding and directly applicable law throughout the Community, overriding national law. The same went for legislation made in exercise of competence conferred by the Treaty. Otherwise, it held, the member states' aim to establish a common market without internal barriers to trade would be unachievable. The cases on the supremacy and direct effect of Community law have been widely recognised as having brought about, in a juridical if not an overtly political sense, the 'constitutionalisation of the treaties'.

Over many years, which saw the accession through five enlargements of a total of nineteen other Member States, each under a freshly agreed treaty of accession, and which saw major treaty revisions (the Single European Act of 1986, the Maastricht Treaty of 1992, that of Amsterdam in 1997, and finally that of Nice in 2000) these judicial decisions stood unamended. What might initially have been set aside, or formally repealed as a kind of judicial *coup d'état* (or *coup de communauté*?) has become a received part of the legal order of the Community and Union. When the 'European Union' was inaugurated in 1992, it was carefully set up outside the Community, which was acknowledged as one of its 'pillars' alongside of two strictly intergovernmental 'pillars' that embraced Foreign and Security Policy, and Justice and Home Affairs. Nevertheless, in the very act of trying thus to encompass and constrain the judicially developed 'constitutional charter' of the Community, the

Treaty on European Union announced the inauguration of citizenship of the Union.[2] This was, as still it will be under the new Constitution, possessed by citizens of all the states as an addition to, not a
substitution for, their national citizenship. So now there was a functional but not yet formal constitution, and there was a common citizenship. Union citizenship was still somewhat shadowy, but the
devising of a common EU form for passports that remain national
passports was an early symbol of the change, and the Court of
Justice began to reflect on the implications of this new citizenship.

The 'basic norm' of the European Union, as of other legal orders,
is no mere juristic hypothesis. The body of custom and usage that
has surrounded acceptance of the Community and Union Treaties,
and acknowledgement of their functionally constitutional character
consequent on the leading ECJ decisions, amounts to a common
acknowledgement of the Treaties' normative status for the Member
States and their citizens. Those who now have the opportunity
actively to embrace that citizenship by an act of political will in
adopting a new Constitution are already citizens (and will remain
so if they decline to adopt it). They are so by virtue of the *acquis
communautaire* whose continuity the preamble and Part IV now
expressly acknowledge. Part III is the vehicle which above all bears
the weight of this *acquis communautaire.* The success of the Union on
which I commented in the prologue, in its contribution to peace,
prosperity, the rule of law and the upholding of human rights,
depended on the building of the single market and the pursuit of the
other treaty-based policies of the union. These are now adapted to
the more democratic framework laid out in Part I, but otherwise
unchanged in their essence. Rejecting the treaty will, again, not take
effect to abolish or change the substance of the policies. All it will do
is to keep them in force within the framework that is blighted by the
democratic deficit.

---

[2]   Compare Weiler, 1999, pp. 230–33

Chapter 6

Do we want a Constitution at all?

Concerns about a Constitution

The current ratification debate, focused in the UK on the referendum, will pose in a stark way the issue whether the Constitution Treaty is a good thing. Does it offer a suitable way to make basic improvements to the legal structure and order of the European Union and its governance? Will such a Constitution help us to make Europe-level laws simpler and more accessible, and to make the Union's institutional system more responsive and transparent? Does the attempt to state concise yet inspiring statements of the Union's aims and objectives succeed? I claim it will, and that even those who wish the UK to leave the EU have no reason to leave it with a confused and undemocratic constitution. The world will be a better place, and the common affairs of the states and citizens of the European union will be more democratically and transparently conducted, also more intelligibly and efficiently, if a better constituted European Union is in being and at work. This is what adoption and implementation of the Constitution seems overwhelmingly likely to achieve. If the United Kingdom or any of its components ever chose to withdraw from the Union, how much better it would be if steps had first been taken to confirm the constitutional power of withdrawal. Such a power is in fact for the first time clearly conferred by Article I-60. A state exercising this power would be able to depart in good will from a Union in whose constitutional improvement it had actively participated. A rejection of the Constitution in the hope of bringing down the whole house of cards would be damaging to Europe and damaging to the UK.

Before we even get to airing those issues in detail, however, a rather urgent prior question may be raised. Is the very idea of a European Constitution acceptable at all, or will it mean the withering away, or even the sudden death of independence and democracy in the states of the Union? Many voices are raised in parliaments and political parties and in the media predicting such a death. They oppose the Constitution, not at the level of detail or internal balance, but absolutely for what it claims to be, a 'constitution' at all. This is a very urgent question to deal with. It is central to the debate in the UK and elsewhere concerning ratification of the 'Treaty Establishing a Constitution for Europe'.

The considerable public concern about this idea in the UK is matched in other countries such as Poland, Denmark, and Sweden. People look anxiously at this great beast of a constitution that has gone slouching to Rome to be born. They find the very idea of a 'Constitution for Europe' deeply troublesome. This is on the ground that a Union with a Constitution must inevitably be or become a super-state that cancels the independence and integrity of the Member States as sovereign entities. These states have been the natural home of democracy, for citizens identify with their state and feel engaged in its affairs. How can this loyalty be transferred to a vast and impersonal 'Europe'? To supersede the state is, they fear, to abandon the very basis of democracy.

I understand this concern, and endorse some of its premises, but do not agree with the conclusion of the argument. If it were sound, it would actually be too late to stop the thing those concerned citizens fear. This is because the Union already has a constitution of the kind concerned citizens and scaremongers in the Euro-sceptic press oppose. This is not a formal 'written constitution'. It is a constitution in substance, not form — what I call a 'functional constitution'. Let me explain this point

Functional and formal constitutions

To understand in what sense the Union has a constitution, you need to grasp this vital distinction: the distinction between a 'constitution in a functional sense' and a 'constitution in a formal sense'. It is a basic conceptual distinction. Let me explain it, starting with the functional sense, which ought to be easy to grasp, since it is the only kind of constitution the UK has.

A constitution in the functional sense exists wherever a self-referential legal order exists. This idea is borrowed with apology and adaptation from the work of two brilliant German scholars, Niklas Luhmann and Günter Teubner. Legal order in itself is not a very problematic idea. It exists whenever there is a set of institutional rules which to a reasonable extent guides the behaviour of a community of people and which they regard as some kind of a unity. Self-reference is more complicated. An order becomes self-referential through the practice of its institutions, and of those other persons who look to the institutions to make rules and decisions by which they will guide their conduct. That practice can reach the point where questions whether there are any valid rules that guide people's conduct come to be considered as questions wholly internal to the particular legal order. Let us take the question whether the Court of Justice of the European Communities currently has power to decide on the binding character of Community law as against states or citizens, or in their favour. The current official answer is 'Yes'. The alternative to this would be that the Court can only view the Treaties as regulating rights and obligations between the different states of Europe. This would leave the states' own Courts and lawmakers to see to it that the rights and obligations of their citizens conform to what is required under Community law (rather in the way in which European Human Rights law works at present).

On this issue, very early in the life of the Community, the Court held that the Treaties on their proper interpretation necessarily implied that the Court did have the power in question. In so holding, they held also that Community law had direct effect in favour of citizens, even against their own state. In due course they held also that Community law as contained in the Treaties had primacy over the law of each member state in the case of any conflict. The same primacy even attached to rules and regulations (directives and regulations, indeed) made by those who could exercise the legislative competence laid down in the Treaty.

A vitally interesting question that comes next is: What made the Court competent to reach these decisions? According to the Court, the Treaty did so. But did it really? That requires interpretation of the Treaty text to tease out its necessary implications. The Court had itself to interpret the Treaty to answer the question. It did so, and also said that Union law had primacy, and the Court necessarily had power to interpret the Treaty to clarify this point. So the Court's interpretation of the Treaty was the basis of the Court's competence. No other judicial authority existed that could correct this in the framework of Community law (though from the point of view of national constitutions, it was challenged, most expressly by the German Constitutional Court). So the most authoritative source for the proposition that the Court has the power it claims is its own decision to that effect.

This is a clear and classical example of self-reference in what was then called Community law, but which will quite soon probably come to be known as 'Union law'. The Court of Justice decides what counts as valid Union law, and how it applies over the head of the national laws of the Member States. The Court can do this because the Court has interpreted the Treaties as authorising it to do so. But of course, that is not all. Over many years up to the present day, all the member states have gone along with this interpretation. Countries like the UK that came in once the Community was well up and running joined a Community which already had this as part of its settled law. In the working legal order of the EU, the powers of the ECJ do not in fact lie solely on the single basis of judicial self-assertion. The other relevant agencies and institutions have accepted these decisions and acted in the spirit of them. They have not denounced them or thrown them out in any of the treaty revisions that have taken place. The character of the legal system of the Union has come to be settled through the custom and usage of those officially engaged in its business, and through at least the acquiescence (and even in some cases the active assent) of most citizens most of the time.

It is itself a legal question to ask who can make law, and how they can make it, as is also the question who decides on the validity and application of laws that are made. To answer these questions authoritatively may depend on authority conferred internally to that very legal order, or not. In the former case, self-referentiality obtains — as it does in Europe.

Within the legal order of the European Union, rules have been established, mainly in the Treaties, but supplemented by case-law and by some secondary legal instruments, that set up the various institutions of the Union. The Commission and the Council of Ministers as set up by these norms exercise the executive power of the Union. The Commission has the right of legislative initiative, and the duty to act as guardian of the Treaties and as supervisor of their faithful implementation by the member states. The legislative power of the Union was originally vested in the Council of Ministers, but has come to be shared with the directly elected European Parliament in all those areas where co-decision obtains (otherwise procedures such as consultation, co-operation, or assent may be required by the treaties). Co-decision now covers a considerable domain — most of single market law, for example.

The judicial power of the Union is principally vested in the Court of Justice. Through the procedure for reference of questions of Community law by state courts to the ECJ, there is a duality of responsibility for judicial implementation of the law in as nearly as possible the same sense throughout the member states. Thus there already are norms that establish and empower institutions to carry out those essential governmental functions that are typically assigned to the trio of executive, legislative and judicial powers. In the exercise of these functions, the appropriate institutions create other norms that directly or indirectly impose obligations or confer rights on legal subjects within the system. The Court of Justice has construed the whole system as being 'of its own kind', *sui generis*, neither international law nor the municipal law of a state.

If I were to assert (as I do) that the United Kingdom has a constitution, it would be on the basis that there is a recognised set of norms that achieve a distribution of powers of an essentially similar kind within a self-referential legal order. The norms in question are varied in their origin, but include the Treaties of Union between Scotland and England and between Great Britain and Ireland (now only Northern Ireland), the legislation that implemented these treaties, other legislation and a great many judicial precedents and constitutional conventions. These compendiously amount to 'the law and custom of the constitution' in a fine old phrase.

The idea of a 'constitution in the functional sense' is nothing other than the set of rules that, taken all together as a dynamic unity, establishes and regulates the self-governance of a political entity. This applies whether the entity you have in mind is a nation state, a union state, a federation, a confederation or whatever other kind of human commonwealth there may be. The norms in question lay down who may exercise what powers, by what formal or informal acts, and subject to what limits. It is a characteristic of the process of implementation and interpretation of a constitution in this sense that, over time, there evolves an ever more dense corpus of constitutional law. This consists both of precedents set by courts and other institutions, and of doctrines and principles developed partly through judicial discourse and partly through the work of scholarly commentators, serious journalists, politicians, statesmen and stateswomen, and others.

The Court of Justice has more than once referred to the foundation Treaties as a 'constitutional charter' of the European Union. Scholars have written of these Court decisions as having achieved the 'constitutionalisation of the Treaties'. For by these decisions, the core provisions of the Treaties dealing with the distribution and limitation of powers became a kind of functional, informal, constitution (see Weiler, 1999; Douglas-Scott, 2002). This explains the point I want to make when I speak of a constitution in the 'functional sense'. The key point is to observe that the constitution in this functional sense is a constitution-in-practice.

Using this terminology and acknowledging the conceptual points made here, you would have to accept this point. Facts similar to those that allow us to say the UK has a constitution in the functional sense force us also to draw the conclusion that in the functional sense, there is already a constitution of the European Union.

There is not, however, a constitution in the formal sense. Let us define this sense. As with the functional sense, a constitution in the formal sense concerns the governance and ordering of a human group, association or polity. As a constitution, it has to establish appropriate institutions of government, and state the powers, the 'competences', that are conferred upon them. It has to declare the limits on these powers, and establish some way of settling boundary disputes about the limits of powers and their legitimate exercise. This is 'formally' achieved when a suitable legal-cum-political instrument is drawn up after deliberation to that end. Such a text must then be solemnly adopted by a formal act of a kind that is ideologically appropriate to the kind of polity or association involved. A formal constitution has to be adopted by an appropriate act, for example, by a referendum vote in a democratic polity, or by ratification of a constitution-treaty by appropriate constitutional acts of States, which in turn might themselves include recourse to a referendum. This is the culmination of a procedure aimed at securing recognition of the text adopted as the basic law, or foundational charter, of the polity whose constitution it purports to be.

On that definition, we may take as settled a second thesis: The European Union does not at present have a constitution in the formal sense. Since 22 June 2003, however, such a formal constitution has been available to it in draft. President Giscard d'Estaing carried the essential Parts I and II of the Convention's text to Thessaloniki on that day and offered it to the European Council as a proposed formal Constitution for the European Union. In turn, after a year's deliberation, the Intergovernmental Conference summoned by the Council adopted a new Treaty that incorporated nearly all of the Convention's draft, modified as we have noted on certain politically sensitive points. The final approved text in all the official languages, signed in Rome on 29 October 2004, is the object to which we address ourselves in the ratification debate. We Europeans have available to us the final text of a formal constitution for the Union, if that is what we choose to have.

Vices and virtues of formal constitutions

The distinction between constitutions in the functional and the formal sense is a real and important one. We may, for example, remind ourselves that many have been the states and unions, for example the Union of Soviet Socialist Republics, that clothed themselves with constitutions in the formal sense. These fully responded to democratic ideas about separation of powers and equal participation of all citizens in political processes, and so forth. But the real political life and functioning of the state or union in question was not regulated by the formal constitution. Nor, therefore, was it explicable in terms of the constitution's formal provisions. The functional constitution diverged to a very substantial degree from the formal text.

Constitutional writers in the United Kingdom, especially in the late nineteenth century, were vigorous critics of what they called 'written constitutions'. They saw that throughout the world of their epoch there were many such constitutions in what is here called the 'formal sense'. These solemnly pronounced separations of powers, declarations of rights and such like, but they actually afforded no shield against despotic or even substantially lawless processes of government. A.V. Dicey (1961), in particular, took the line that a constitution like the British constitution as he conceptualised it, consisting in practices of Crown, Parliament and the Courts underpinned by a genuinely effective common law tradition, worked more satisfactorily to the end of ordered liberty than any of the formal constitutions.

In the circumstances of the time when he was writing, Dicey was right both about the true prevalence of liberty under a satisfactory constitution in the functional sense (putting the point in my terms) and about the dismal record of many, though by no means all, formal constitutions. The English constitutional tradition to which he contributed so massively has cast a long shadow over attitudes in the UK to constitutional politics. This continues down to the present day, giving rise to a peculiarly English — English much more than British — nervousness about the very idea of adopting a European constitution.

One point of incontestable weight survives in any event from Dicey's reflections. Putting it in terms of the distinction between functional and formal constitution, it is this: a satisfactory functional constitution, even without any formal text formally adopted, is preferable to a dysfunctional formal constitution. This is especially so when the existence of a formal constitution acts as an ideological cover-up for despotic or otherwise undesirable governmental activity.

What that does not mean is that formal constitutions themselves are undesirable or dangerous. On the contrary, where there is a formal constitution with satisfactorily liberal-democratic provisions for the polity in question, and where the practice of those in office in its various branches conforms to the ideals of the constitution and to the restrictions it lays down on the exercise of power, there is both a constitution in the formal sense and a matching functional constitution. This is highly desirable, because in such a case there is a great deal more transparency about the conduct of government.

The citizen who wishes to know how the polity runs itself can read the constitution and be enlightened by it, especially in the light of further commentaries about constitutional practice and usage. This tends to be the case whenever the formal constitution is fully observed as the functioning basis of legal and political order. Perhaps the growth of conventions and parts of constitutional law dependent on precedent might make the functional constitution somewhat more extensive in reach than the text of the formal constitution would suggest. But that would not matter and would indeed replicate common experience. Meantime, it is important to repeat what was said in Chapter 3 about the 'core constitution' that is stated in the quite short and straightforward Part I of the Constitution. This is far more intelligible to the ordinary person than the convoluted texts of the existing Treaties.

There is already a functional constitution of the Union, and its provisions can be discerned within the Treaties as supplemented by judicial interpretations of them. But nobody outside professional governmental or specialist-legal or academic circles really understands it. No wonder there is a fair amount of alienation from the Union. To pay off this serious intelligibility deficit, there is a very good case for adopting the formal constitution now on offer.

In so far as the existing 'functional constitution' of the Union came into being by stealth and as a result of judicial rather than popular decision-making, the present constitution lacks full democratic legitimacy (see Booker and North, 2002, pp. 134–57). The process of adopting this Constitution, if it goes forward successfully, will redeem that legitimacy deficit. By democratic means the Union will have adopted a Constitution that enhances democracy in its own governance. This will not abolish the present special character of the Union (discussed in the next chapter), but can mark the first effective marrying of democratic institutions with the principles of confederal self-government as contrasted with those of full-dress federalism. This will have been done by the only way in which constitutional arrangements can successfully develop, namely by immanent critique guiding incremental improvement in already evolving institutions and rules.

Chapter 7

Will the EU become a superstate if the Constitution is adopted?

Let me continue the argument about the special character of the Union. It is not reasonable to regard the currently existing European Union as a 'state' or a 'super state'. It is a multi-state union of its own kind that involves a sharing and pooling of certain sovereign powers to achieve the determined common aims of the Union, while respecting the constitutional integrity of its members. They in turn have their own constitutional orders that interact with and necessarily dovetail with the EU system. But they are not derivative from it — they retain constitutional independence in a condition that I have dubbed 'constitutional pluralism'(MacCormick, 1999; Douglas-Scott, 2002, pp. 523–30). (For the functional constitution of the Union is not a subordinate offshoot of any particular state's constitution, far less of all of them compendiously; nor is the validity of any state's constitution derived from that of the Union.) A union of this novel and distinctive form exhibits some of the characteristics of classical federal unions, some of those of international organisations, and some of the ideal type of a confederation. By a 'confederation', I mean an arrangement in which the governments of a group of states acting together in a regulated way participate in common institutions for the collective government of the whole.

The prospect of adopting a formal Constitution for the European Union seems to me therefore to be less alarming than many opponents make it seem. If having a constitution entails being a state, then the EU is already a state, since it already has a constitution in at least the functional sense. Opting for a formal as well as functional constitution will not change that, though it will help to make the whole scheme intelligible to politically interested citizens. If the kind of state so constituted would be a super-state, then the EU would have to be already a super-state. But in fact the EU is not a state, nor, therefore a super-state. And if as things stand now the EU is not a super-state (or any kind of state), then there is nothing to fear from a formal constitution as such. Certainly, opponents of super-statehood will rightly concern themselves with ensuring that the proposed constitution does not adopt forms that deprive the Union of its present 'suigenericity', its novel own-kind character as a grand experiment in the construction of a transnational polity. But making a clearer formal constitution for this 'suigeneric' Union is in itself a perfectly sensible thing to do.

Why do I say the European Union is not a state but a polity of its own kind, '*sui generis*' as latinists put it?. The answer, for which I am indebted to former Irish Prime Minister John Bruton, is that it lacks certain essential characteristics of statehood. For a start, it has no monopoly of legitimate force over the Union's territory, but depends on the states to apply and enforce its laws. Nor has it independent tax raising powers, being dependent on the states for all its 'own resources'. Nor may it run a budget deficit (indeed, its ceiling of allowable expenditure, as already noted, is set at 1.28% of the GDP of the Union, in contrast to the USA which spends about 20% at the Federal level). It can co-ordinate the defence of the Union but cannot raise a defence force of its own. Some key parts of its arrangements do not apply throughout the territories belonging to the Union — for example, the eurozone is not co-extensive with EU, even though the euro is the official currency of the Union (Article I-8).[1] In future, moreover, in areas that may include defence, states

---

[1]   THE SYMBOLS OF THE UNION
- The flag of the Union shall be a circle of twelve golden stars on a blue background.
- The anthem of the Union shall be based on the 'Ode to Joy' from the Ninth Symphony by Ludwig van Beethoven.
- The motto of the Union shall be: 'United in diversity'.
- The currency of the Union shall be the euro.

will be able to engage under the constitution in projects for enhanced co-operation, proceeding with further integration more rapidly than can be achieved by unanimity. The Union co-exists with its Member States in a condition of 'constitutional pluralism' under which each state retains its own constitutional independence, including the right of exit from the Union. On the other hand, the constitutional character of the Union has already been developed autonomously by judicial interpretation, in a manner that will probably not be undercut by the terms of Article I-1 and the 'principle of conferral'. For that is the twin of the 'principle of primacy of Union law', which derives from the early constitutionalising decisions of the Court of Justice (Weiler, 1999, pp. 16–39).

It is reasonable to conclude that the Union is a hybrid polity, having some elements of the federal and some of an international organisation of a particularly intimate kind, aspiring to effective democratic self-government at several levels guided by the principle of subsidiarity. The suigenericity of the Union should be welcomed and cherished. If 'confederation' is not too shop-soiled a term, it perhaps fits the Union better than any alternative. Once the Treaty Establishing a Constitution for Europe is ratified and is in force (if it ever is), the text thus adopted will become in plain and simple terms 'the Constitution' that guides the working reality of the Union. For that is how it refers to itself internally in the text. Its amendment will be regulated by itself (under Part IV), in a way that reflects the confederal or suigeneric character of the Union, still requiring large-scale consensus, but giving special significance to any amendments adopted by at least four fifths of the states. The quality of the constitution should be judged by its contents, not by the legal act, that of Treaty-making, that brought it into being as a project for ratification.

Chapter 8

Is European-scale democracy possible at all?

A key point of my argument throughout has harped on about making the European Union democratic, or, at least, more democratic than it is at present. I have suggested that the improved and more open two-chamber legislative procedure, with improved consultation of national parliaments also, will mark a step forward in democracy. I will say the same about enhanced answerability of the Commission to the European Parliament, and the linkage between the election of the President of the Commission and the outcome of European Parliamentary elections. This ties in with an overall idea about a generally more effective democratic accountability of law-makers and other decision-makers.

This will be much enhanced by the Constitution's provisions, particularly those brought together in Part I, Title 6, on 'the Democratic Life of the Union', and in Title 7 on budgetary and financial provisions. The directly elected European Parliament will become an almost all-purpose participant in every legislative act of the Union (a very few are reserved for enactment by Council with Parliament's assent, and the provisions about regulating the Parliament itself are to converse effect). It will also acquire power over approval of the whole budget, with no special exception for 'compulsory expenditure' that effectively ring-fences agricultural spending at the expense of all other heads of expenditure. At the same time, the Council of Ministers, as one house of what is now acknowledged to be effectively a two-chamber legislature, must deliberate and vote in public whenever it is engaged in law-making. Its agenda will be divided to separate non-legislative from legislative business. (See Articles I-46, I-50; this reform is already anticipated since the Seville Council of 2002). Moreover, arrangements (still to be discussed) under the Subsidiarity Protocol will involve Member State parliaments in before-the-event scrutiny of Union legislation in draft. These proposed arrangements have considerable potential to enhance real democratic accountability in parliaments all over the Union, before ministers set off to the Council to do their legislative business.

Provisions concerning the election of the President and Members of the Commission, and their dismissal, will enhance the already considerable degree to which the Commission is really answerable to the European Parliament. Yet it will not become the kind of parliament-based executive that can hog-tie parliamentary accountability so effectively as can governments under constitutional arrangements like those of the UK. The fate of the Santer Commission and now, most recently, the rejected nomination of Mr Buttiglione as Commissioner for Justice and Home Affairs, indicate the degree to which Parliament can exert and sustain pressure on the Commission as well as freely amending legislative drafts brought forward by the Commission. The European Parliament is less visible but can exercise much more initiative of its own than can the UK Parliament, in respect of which democratic accountability has really become more a matter of five-yearly accountability of the Executive to the electorate via parliamentary elections than effective day-by-day control of the executive by the legislature.

Taking account of all this, and reminding ourselves of the significance of the Charter as part II of the Constitution, we can fairly conclude that the scheme of government envisaged in the Draft Constitution is, beyond doubt, limited government. The limitations, albeit elaborate, seem fully intelligible and quite workable. This Constitution offers a blueprint for a scheme of government within Europe that is both limited and democratically answerable. It does so by building on the better parts of what has been inherited, and extending the reach of the best parts. It does not do so in a spirit of 'constructivist rationalism' as though it were possible to cure all human ills according to a perfectly designed blueprint imagined out of nothing.

During the period I spent working as an elected representative in the European Parliament, I became more, not less, impressed with the democratic potentialities of the European institutional set-up. This was especially due to the growing role of Parliament in co-decision. It owed even more to the relative independence of action each MEP enjoys as a constituency representative with the kind of party political responsibilities nearly all elected officials have in large scale schemes of representative democracy, but with very weak transnational party discipline. It also reflected the new confidence that Parliament acquired during the struggle for accountability of the Commission under the presidency of Jacques Santer.

There are many widely current misapprehensions about the European Parliament, due among other things to the tiny coverage the mass media give to its activities, particularly in the UK but also very largely in other Member States. I have often read that it works 'by consensus' rather than by adversarial arguments. This is a half-falsehood, rather than a half-truth. Since there is not a government party of left or of right whose prime task is to support the government and help to secure passage of its legislation, there is no single government-versus-opposition axis of adversarial argument. But there are often issues that divide parliament in a broadly left–right way, or that raise issues on a different axis of division, for example concerning environmental or consumer issues, or small innovative businesses versus established giants, or regional versus centralist interests. Different national political traditions and commercial practices impinge on, or are affected, differentially by proposed European legislation. This means that both in Committee (where most of the detailed argument takes place well beyond the curiosity of most of the already small media corps) and in Plenary Session there is often vigorous and even passionate argument. Votes are based on voting lists prepared by Parliament's political groups. But none has an overall majority on its own, and there can frequently be differences of opinion inside Groups, based on national party views or other bases of political sympathy. In the upshot, there is considerable fluidity of voting issue by issue, and a majority that prevails in one vote may fail to hold out for the next. Most MEPs find themselves acting with real judgement and discretion, not as blind lobby fodder. Outcomes may reflect compromises, but these are often multi-party compromises. MEPs have to be very much alive to the impact of proposed legislation on significant bodies of interest in their own constituency, and loyalty to the European Group is readily trumped by constituency loyalty. This makes the role of MEP correspond very much more closely to the classical Burkean idea of the role of a representative charged with exercising judgement rather then a mere agent carrying out a fixed mandate. Certainly, there can be issues – often issues concerning the internal management of the Parliament and the distribution of offices in it — on which the two largest Groupings of Centre Right (European People's Party and European Democrats) and Centre Left (Party of European Socialists) make a deal. Then they can outvote all the rest easily. But this is not an everyday occurrence, and in other circumstances the Centre Party (currently, 'Group of Liberals and Democrats for Europe'), or the Greens/European Free Alliance and other smaller groupings, can exercise decisive influence individually or in momentary alliances. This is apart from the weight that individual MEPs' arguments may have carried during deliberations in Committee.

Even if all that were conceded, and some virtue conceded to the European Parliament and its (mainly) hard-working Members, there are thinkers who would deny that it does or can add up to anything properly considered to be 'democracy'. There is a family of arguments that cluster around the claim that the circumstances of democracy do not now exist and cannot come into existence in the EU in the early, or, perhaps, the foreseeable, future. One way of putting this argument rests on the etymology of the term 'democracy' — this derives from the Greek words meaning rule by the *demos*, the people. But there is not, it is said, a Europe-wide *demos*, or *Volk*, or people. Without this, nothing can be said to be in place to exercise the rule of the many rather than of the few. In earlier times, the few were the aristocrats. Nowadays they are the bureaucrats, who act in the name of the common good but cannot really have it authenticated by any true representatives of the many. For what exists is not a single people but a patchwork of many peoples, among each of which — in the Member States, of course — true democracy can prevail (Grimm, 1995).

Another, perhaps less mysterious, way of expressing this objection refers not to a *demos* but to a 'political class'(Siedentop, 2000) a body of citizens interested and engaged in questions of public affairs, who conceive of themselves as participating in debate over common issues with others likewise concerned. Within such a class there is likely to be at least broad consensus or communality of opin-ion about what is currently on the political agenda and what are the main arguments to be considered, or what are the contending ideo-logical stances. Not a single set but at least a set of overlapping sets of concepts and terms-in-use will be shared but also contested among members of such a class. Democratic institutions are the focus of the debates in which members of a political class engage using such concepts and terms and addressing a loosely shared agenda from time to time. No such class, however, exists in Europe. There is not a European political class with shared press and broadcast media and a common language of debate.

Even when debate is about all-Europe issues, it will be carried on in French on RTF or in *Le Monde* or *le Figaro*, or in Italian in one of the bewilderingly many media outposts controlled by Mr Berlusconi, or in German, or Polish, or English or Swedish or Spanish. All this will go on without very much regard to what is being said in other languages through other media. When European Parliamentary elections take place, they seldom focus on the great issues facing Europe, or even the middle-ranking issues currently under debate in the European Parliament. State-by-state the voters vote on issues currently in controversy in the state's own politics and parliament — often, this will be a way of expressing a mid-term verdict on the present government rather than any kind of considered judgement about a common European good.

Yet another way to put this is to say that there is neither European society nor a European public mind (Allott 2002, sections 6.26-6.32). There might have been a kind of grand society of societies at the all-Europe level, but the development first of the EEC and then of a European Union that incorporates the European Community as one of its 'pillars' has actually defeated this. Intergovernmental Europe locked on to the bureaucratic Europe of the Commission and its Directorates-General reduces Europe to an elaborate system of ongoing horse-trades and pork-barrels (or wine lakes and butter mountains). This has shifted key decisions out of democratic home rule in the member States and illicitly over-empowered the execu-tive branches of the states sitting doing deals in Brussels at Council, COREPER and the like.

I have one great difficulty with all these arguments. They make radically unintelligible things that actually happen, things I have seen happening. The European Parliament is a far from perfect institution — but it does rather well the job I have described. It does achieve a genuinely popular-representative element in the legislative process of Europe. It ensures that minorities, whether Roma people or Azorean or Hebridean or Shetlander fishing people or small scale computer software developers or credit union participants in the North of England, central Scotland and Ireland do not go unheard, just to take some recent examples. Great issues are also handled in a variety of ways, like the (clearly all-Europe) problem of halting environmental degradation, or sustaining a single market without denuding consumers of fair legal protection. If 'compulsory expenditure' on the Common Agricultural Policy is abolished with entry into force of the Constitution, the question of the balance of need between agricultural support and other needs for expenditure in pursuit of the objectives of the European Union will become open to Parliamentary debate and vote.

None of this requires the being-in-existence already of a single *demos*, or political class, or self-conscious society with one public mind. We are back to the older problem of trying to hold factions in check, to secure that no single interest group or national interest can capture a process of decision-making that is supposed to act on behalf of everyone. The mosaic quality of the European Parliament and its always-shifting majority item by item and vote by vote is a very good control for the purpose of screening against take-over by any particular faction or sectional interest. It reminds one of the greater wisdom, perhaps, of Aristotle than of contemporary theorists. The 'common good' is not some set of circumstances specifiable in advance of a debate and a collective decision-making process. It is in a certain sense both constituted and discovered in the process of a debate in which many voices can be heard and none can hope to have their position viewed with sympathy if they ignore differing positions of others. It is an emergent concept, not a target for pursuit by a *demos*, a political class, or a society.

Perhaps I will be accused of confusing real democracy with merely representative government engaged in the compromising of partly conflicting interests. My crude reply would be that there is actually a lot to be said for representative government that achieves a compromise among partly conflicting interests. Representative government of this kind acquires a genuinely democratic element when the representatives are elected on a basis of one-person-one-vote with universal franchise in reasonably defined constituencies. Exact equality of voting weight can reasonably be qualified with a measure of 'degressive proportionality' applied to ensure that the smallest constituencies (smallest Member States, in Europe's case) do not lose out in the expression of their own internal pluralism. This is perhaps overdone when you reach the point at which a country like Wales has but four representatives in the European Parliament balanced against six for a state as small as Malta. This is certainly a blemish in the final version of the Constitution. But blemishes apart, the representative character of the Parliament remains, as does the popular and tolerably equal basis of the franchise.

A stronger sense of peoplehood, however, or of common citizenship, and an emergent political class may over time develop around representative institutions having the character of those that exist now. Such a sense is more likely to prove to be a consequence of the nurturing of representative institutions that remain imperfectly democratic at the all-Europe level, from the point of view of one or another ideal conception of democracy. Certainly, it would do nothing to foster the emergence of such a democracy if the functional constitution is left as it is at present, with the kind of upshot to which I drew attention in respect of the European Arrest Warrant in the Prologue to this book.

This view can be tied in to a very important idea put forward by Jürgen Habermas. This concerns the possibility of 'constitutional patriotism' (Habermas, 1992). Human polities need not be grounded simply in the bonds of mutual sympathy, arising from a real or imagined common ethnicity or common language. You can share things other than ethnicity and culture. You can, for example, share a constitution, for example by all voting to adopt it. Humans who do share a constitution, and who are satisfied to take part in the political community it defines, can be drawn together precisely by their common loyalty to the constitution — or, rather, the constitutional and legal order that unfolds in accordance with it.

This could be all the more so when a constitutional order in a previously evolved and currently not very satisfactory shape is used as the launch-pad for a new, more intelligible and democratic constitution to be adopted only if enough of the already-citizens vote to embrace it. Such citizens could thus acquire a newly and more substantially defined citizenship (Charter of Rights, etc) defined by this new constitution that a critical debate before, at, and after the Convention has distilled out of the current one.

If the citizens do so, they will endorse a legislative process that has proper democratic legitimation in the Parliament and in the Council under scrutiny of national parliaments, with a more fully accountable Executive than hitherto. Given the formula for Qualified Majority voting in the Council (55% of states, representing 65% of all citizens, but no blocking minority to comprise fewer than four states) and the need for an absolute majority of votes in the Parliament, checks and balances abound. If, as discussed in the next but one chapter, subsidiarity and proportionality are adequately defined and policed, the little democracies of the locality, the city, the region, the stateless nation, will be left to do the things that are best done with local commitment and local knowledge. The Member States as contexts of very strong democratic identification will not suffer undue intrusion from the European legislature thrusting on them unwanted and unnecessary legislation that burdens domestic law with unnecessary trappings from transnational busibodies.

In these circumstances, Europeans who reflect on the imperatives for common and continuing peace in decent prosperity in this continent, for achievement of a satisfactory and sustainable environment both continentally and globally, and for a fair contribution to the prosperity of developing countries, may not see the European Union as a looming and threatening super-state, a 'country called Europe'. If so, this Union will then be able to call forth patriotism around a suigeneric constitution for a democratic confederation unparalleled in the World's history to date.

Chapter 9

Accountable executives?

For those who believe in the old idea of a 'mixed constitution', the element lacking in the European Union's constitutional set-up has been that of the 'monarch', the leading figure who personifies and energises the executive achievements of a polity. Such a figure need not of course occupy an hereditary office, indeed could not do so in present democratic times. The Constitution provides a power in the European Council to nominate a President of the Commission to the European Parliament following each European election, the nominee being subject to election or rejection by the Parliament. This will improve the democratic legitimacy of the Commission, for the election of the President is bound to reflect the weight of political opinion expressed in the election. (The Council does indeed make a nomination to Parliament, but, if there were a clear majority position in Parliament, the Council would be no more able to ignore this than can the monarch in the UK ignore an election result when inviting a new Prime Minister to take office.)

Once the first, or a subsequent, acceptable nominee is elected, this new President and the Council will 'by common accord' agree a list of nominee Commissioners, and the whole Commission will be subject to a 'vote of consent' by the European Parliament. Any member of the Commission must resign if requested to do so by the President, who otherwise has extensive powers to oversee the organisation and working of the Commission. The first Commission to take office under the Constitution will contain one citizen from each of the member states, but thereafter the number will be equivalent to two thirds of the total of the member states, in a sub-set exhibiting appropriate geographical and other diversity.

Each state will over time have equality with every other in respect of the frequency of being represented among the membership of the Commission. Members of the Commission are decidedly required not to be or act as representatives of states in any other sense. Their constitutionally prescribed role is to uphold the Constitution and laws made under it and to act for the general European interest. It is nevertheless important that citizens in all the states be confident over time that the Commission acts on the basis of a real understanding of the circumstances of life and the political and constitutional tradition of each state. That is the point of the rotation around states on equal terms, with a two-thirds rule governing the size of the Commission (e.g., when the Union has twenty seven members, the Commission will be eighteen strong). The hope underlying this proposal is that it will be found to allow for sufficient sensitivity in the Commission to the diversity of the union, while assuring sufficient cohesiveness to provide effective government.

Ideally, at least, the Commission works as a government of many talents, transnational in composition and politically a coalition rather than a Party government. The Commission has at present and retains under the Constitution the main power of legislative initiative, but the power to make the laws in response to these proposals is exercised by the Parliament and the Council of Ministers. Its President will be something rather more than *primus inter pares*, for he has the power to call for the resignation of other Commissioners, and directs the work of the whole college. A President so elected and empowered will be a figure of real and substantial authority in the Union and in the wider world, without becoming a first citizen in the style of a President of the USA, or of France.

Does it risk confusion or conflict that the constitution also provides for a new full-time Presidency of the European Council? For a term of two and a half years renewable, the European Council will elect its own President, who may not be a person holding any national office. Will a President in this position not overshadow the role of the Commission President? Is this no more than a recipe for confusing citizens and outsiders alike? Who speaks for the Union? There is a real matter of concern here, but it is worth noticing that the Draft Constitution gives the Council Presidency quite restricted functions, and nothing like the authority over members of the Council than the Commission President has over its members. The chairing of the European Council is an important task, and so is that

of securing a continuity of the agenda and monitoring the follow-up
of its successive meetings, as well as checking on progress of work
at the Council of Ministers.. There will in addition be a figurehead
role to play in external relations[1]. But it remains the case that the
President of the European Council will be a figure who does not
hold, or no longer holds, any national mandate, but is elected to the
Chair by the votes of those who do.

Chairing a body all of whose members hold continuing office as
head of government or executive head of state, this President will
hold a position far short of *primus inter pares*. Indeed, as I remarked
in a debate in the European parliament on 19 June 2003, 'less than
par inter primos' seems a more appropriate description. There is a
real contrast with the substantial constitutional authority vested in
the President of the Commission. It may turn out on occasion that
the Council invites the President of the Commission to take its chair,
and this could even some day grow into a convention of the Constitution. That would, at any rate, be one way to avoid the risk of conflicting authorities, or their puzzling appearance from the citizen's
point of view.

In strategic terms, and especially in relation to Foreign and Security policy, the European Council has a vital role. The proposed Foreign Minister of the Union, who will also hold office as a Vice
President of the Commission, will play a key part in maintaining
coherence between Council and Commission. Through the European Council, and also in relation to the Council of Ministers, a balance will be maintained with the Member States and their
Parliaments, whose monitoring role will have been strengthened in
the way noted above. The extension of the ordinary legislative process (formerly 'co-decision') to the great majority of the legislative
functions of the Union likewise strengthens the role of the European
Parliament. There do, however, remain some doubts concerning the
balance of authority as between Council and Commission. The fact
that it would be possible to merge the two Presidencies (if it came to
seem desirable) by appointing one person to both of them might be
a solution if difficulties emerge. If not, there will have proven to be

---

[1]   See Article I-21 (2). The task of 'assuring the external representation of the
      Union' (but without prejudice to the functions of the Union Minister for
      Foreign Affairs) gives the figurehead element to this function, but the rest
      of the Article simply underlines that the President's functions are
      co-ordinating and chairing, not exercising executive authority. Contrast
      Article I-26 dealing with the Commission Presidency.

no confusion of executive roles between Commission and Council and their respective presidencies.

Yet again, we can conclude that the proposals do contain risks and potential difficulties. These are not ones that lie beyond the reach of human ingenuity. The degree of democratic accountability and transparency is increased under the proposals. The balance of advantage lies with giving them a try.

Chapter 10

What is subsidiarity, and why does it matter?

Connected to the questions we discussed about the conditions for European democracy is the issue of subsidiarity. An important test of the Constitution is whether or not it deals satisfactorily with the need to avoid over-centralisation. Lawmakers have a natural tendency to make laws on anything over which they have competence — but in most areas of Union activity, competence is shared between the Union's institutions and the Member States. The competences retained by the Member States in turn include competences exercisable not by the central institutions of the state but by constitutionally empowered *Länder* or autonomous nationalities or regions, or devolved nations having their own legislative competence. Moreover, legislation, for example on environmental issues, can have a considerable impact on the exercise of other competences right down to the most local level.

For example, a rural local authority may find the task of collecting disused refrigerators very much more expensive per item collected than an urban one, most so in areas of least dense population. The Union has no power in relation to the provision of primary and secondary education, or over expenditure on local highways in the Member States. But those who do have responsibility for these matters may find that the budgetary impact of meeting environmental liabilities arising under Union law about, say, discarded refrigerators, affects their ability to maintain what they consider a suitable level of expenditure on schools or highways.

Considerations of this kind draw to our attention the issue of subsidiarity. The concept emerges from Catholic moral theology, and from the doctrine that 'subsidium', or support by the state's authorities, should be extended to individuals and families only to the extent that they are unable to provide for themselves. Taken in a wider sense, it implies that more general levels of government should intervene in matters of social concern only to the extent that less general, more local ones cannot do so to a sufficient degree, and so on right down the line to the family itself. The idea was adapted and adopted into Community law by the Maastricht Treaty, and achieves its latest formulation in Article I-11 (3) of the Constitution:

> Under the principle of subsidiarity, in areas which do not fall within its exclusive competence, the Union shall act only if and insofar as the objectives of the proposed action cannot be sufficiently achieved by the Member States, either at central level or at regional and local level, but can rather, by reason of the scale or effects of the proposed action, be better achieved at Union level.

The innovation achieved by this new formulation is the introduction — for which quite a few of us pressed at the Convention — of reference to the 'regional and local level', a point to which we shall return in a later chapter. More important still is the revised Protocol concerning the implementation of the principle. The second paragraph of section 3 of Artcle I-11 obliges the institutions of the Union to observe this principle in accordance with the Protocol, and also empowers national parliaments to supervise its application. The Protocol apples also to the Principle of Proportionality, save that in this case national parliaments have no supervisory function, proportionality being defined as follows in section 4 of I-11:

> Under the principle of proportionality, the content and form of Union action shall not exceed what is necessary to achieve the objectives of the Constitution.

Unlike the principle of subsidiarity, that of proportionality applies to the exclusive as well as the non-exclusive competences of the Union. But in relation to exclusive competences, it should be noted that elements within these can be delegated back to the states by the Union. Since the principle of subsidiarity does not apply, there is no duty on the Union to delegate back, even in cases where tasks could be better achieved locally. Aspects of marine biological resource conservation under the Common Fisheries Policy could be cited as a case in point.

The Protocol imposes on the Commission, the Council, the Parliament, and Member States a duty not to undertake legislative proposals, or to bring forward draft legislative acts, unless they are satisfied that they are compatible with the principles of subsidiarity and proportionality. The authority responsible for a particular draft act must undertake full pre-legislative consultation, taking due account of any regional and local dimension of a proposal. It must then attach to each legislative proposal a sufficiently detailed statement on subsidiarity to make possible a judgement whether the constitutional principle is satisfied in this case. Account must be taken of possible legislative, administrative, or budgetary burdens to be borne by regional and local authorities and also 'economic operators and citizens', and anticipated benefits should be shown to be proportionate to costs incurred.

Provision is made both for political and for judicial policing of these requirements. Proportionality is well established as a justiciable principle, and the ECJ and national courts are well able to appraise legislation on this account. Subsidiarity is manifestly more open textured, requiring value judgements of a difficult kind. Nevertheless, it will be possible for a Court to scrutinise a statement by the Commission (for example) justifying some proposal to take Union-wide legislative action, and to assess whether it really fulfils the requirements laid down in the Protocol. If so, it will also be possible to review whether legislation as proposed by the Commission or as finally enacted by Parliament and Council could reasonably be deemed justified in the light of the subsidiarity statement that accompanied the original draft.

In ordinary practice, though, the political controls will almost certainly be more salient, though they would be much less valuable without the judicial long-stop. Each draft act by the Commission or other empowered authority is to be delivered directly to each Member State parliament, with a six-week delay before the Union legislative process takes its next step. Each Parliament, or each chamber of each parliament where bicameral legislatures exist, will have the opportunity to scrutinise the proposed legislation and to submit to the Union institutions a reasoned opinion protesting that the proposal violates the principle of subsidiarity. This would involve showing how the proposed Union legislation cuts into areas of shared competence on matters which it would be more appropriate to regulate by legislation at central or regional level within the state.

Any such reasoned opinions must be delivered to and taken into account by Commission, Council and Parliament. When up to a third of votes available to state parliaments (two for single-chamber parliaments, one per chamber of bicameral parliaments) is cast in favour of a protest on subsidiarity grounds, or up to a quarter where proposals concern the area of freedom, security and justice, the Commission (or other authority) must review its proposal. Thereafter, it may, upon stated reasons, maintain, amend, or withdraw its proposal.

It seems highly probable that, in cases in which the Commission (for example) maintains its proposal for stated reasons, these reasons will be subjected to especially critical scrutiny. The option of invoking the Court of Justice will be quite likely to be taken up if the reasons seem inadequate or question-begging. For parliaments as well as the executive governments of member states are effectively empowered under the Protocol to raise actions concerning infringement of subsidiarity. (The state's government will be required to formally adopt for submission to the Court any complaint its Parliament (or a chamber of it) wants to have tested judicially.)

Some commentators have derided the political controls. They think it too trivial that the controls ultimately require the Commission (or other authority) to do no more than 'review' a proposal, but permit it, when it thinks fit, to 'maintain' a proposal. This it can do in the face of protests from as many as a quarter or two thirds of member state parliaments. There is a risk, here, however, that we overlook the real political and juridical possibilities. Whether or not a proposal is maintained, it still has to be enacted, with possible amendments, by Council and Parliament. It will never be easy to achieve a qualified majority in Council and an overall majority in Parliament in the face of substantial opposition expressed through national parliaments which represent the very citizens by whom MEPs are elected. Ministers in Council will also be aware of the level of opposition they face at home. Even when majorities are available to press legislation through to a conclusion, the aggrieved Parliaments retain their right of access to the Court of Justice. There, it will be necessary to produce copper-bottomed arguments showing that the reasoned opinions of the protesting parliaments are mistaken. It will have to be shown convincingly that there really is a job to be done in pursuit of an objective of the Union that the member states cannot achieve, even through local but co-ordinated action, either at central or at regional level.

Where a substantial number of regional authorities is engaged in protest against legislative proposals on topics on which the Committee of the Regions has a constitutional right to be consulted, they will be able to activate that Committee. For this purpose, the Protocol empowers the Committee to challenge legislation before the Court of Justice on grounds of violation of subsidiarity. Additionally, regional parliaments may have the opportunity to activate votes by a chamber of the national parliament such as the *Bundesrat*, or to interact with the central parliament, as may the Scottish Parliament or the National Assembly for Wales in the UK. It is even possible for regional parliaments to be deemed to act as the Member State parliament for all matters in their own competence, as will be the case in Belgium. Under the new Constitution (if it is adopted) the Union will clearly have to be yet more alert than previously to the impact of all-union measures on the freedom of local and regional authorities to apply local knowledge to sensibly regulating matters of general concern in a locally sensitive way.

One rather fruitless controversy which surfaced during the constitutional debate was on the issue whether subsidiarity is or could become a legal concept, not simply the name for a highly subjective political desideratum. Is 'subsidiarity' properly interpreted as a legal principle guiding political decision-making, or is it really pure politics? There is a lot of room for disagreement about when an objective can or cannot be 'sufficiently' achieved at one level of government rather than at another. Likewise, on the question what or how much can 'by reason of the scale or effects of the proposed action, be better achieved at Union level'. The front-line judges of such questions are, inevitably, politicians and civil servants, both the (more) centrally based ones who see advantage in a single scheme applicable everywhere and the (more) locally based ones who desire appropriate discretion to ensure that large scale objectives and proposals are sensibly tailored to local circumstances and attitudes. If, however, the politicians alone undertake the judgement of such matters, the question inevitably arises which of them is to be final judge, all being in some sense judges in their own cause. For that reason it is essential that there be some impartial adjudicator, in this case the ECJ, in relation to which there must be a sufficiently articulated constitutional standard by reference to which the

Court can ensure that the principle is being fairly upheld. A Court's judgement on this is of course a judgement about politics, concerning the proper conduct of those having political duties to perform, and concerning a value of great importance to the polity in question. But it need not be, and ought not to be, a partisan political judgement rather than an impartial judicial one guided by a reasonable conception of the concept applied.

In terms of the objective of enhancing the democratic character of government in the Union, the Subsidiarity Protocol and the closely connected Protocol on the Role of National Parliaments in the European Union have great significance. Previously, it has been required that legislative drafts, green papers, statements of annual legislative programmes, and agenda for and minutes of the Council in its legislative functions be submitted to the Governments of the Member States. They made their own arrangements to pass them on to other official and unofficial consultees in parliaments and outside of them. Now they will go directly to parliaments as well, with required delays before legislative action on a draft commences at Union level (except in cases of urgency, for which reasons must be stated). Previously, it was up to governments to keep parliaments informed, under the influence of an intergovernmental conception of the Union. In future, parliaments will themselves be informed as of right.

This will facilitate, without forcing, increased parliamentary scrutiny of Union legislation while it is still in draft. It will enhance the effective answerability of ministers individually and governments collectively for the decisions they make or participate in at the Council. It will facilitate debate on the general policy line a government takes about the desirability of regulating this or that matter at all-Union level, and if so, whether by laws or framework laws. In the latter case, debate will also focus on how much discretion a framework law on the given subject matter should leave to the states and their regions adequately to take account of special local circumstances. You can, as is well known, take a horse to water, but cannot make it drink. To the extent that there is a head of steam of democratic discontent about excessively remote figures in the European Institutions undertaking excessively intrusive legislative acts bearing on the lives of citizens, a better remedy than before is at hand. It remains to be seen how assiduously parliaments will use it.

It will be up to members of parliaments, goaded, perhaps, by frustrated citizens, to ensure that they fully exploit the provisions that facilitate their intervention in issues of subsidiarity, and also of general legislative policy. It is not likely to be sufficient simply to have specialised European Affairs committees that scrutinise legislative drafts from the Union level. Other specialist subject committees such as those of, for example, the Scottish Parliament, must routinely be kept fully informed about draft European legislation and, in due course, about its progress through the Union legislative process. This alone will enable them to ask the right questions at the right time — the right question being whether any of the legislation, or any of its details, crosses the line over which better judgement can be exercised locally than centrally. A specialist committee dealing regularly with justice and home affairs, or with fisheries, has a better basis for judgement of that issue in these domains than a generalist European Committee, however well-serviced. Of course, the overview taken by European Affairs committees (under whatever name) will always be important also. A Europe of active parliamentary scrutiny at all levels will be a more responsively democratic Europe than anything we have seen hitherto. Whichever level of government seems to a citizen most materially to represent her or him, there should be a point of entry there to raise concerns about legislative proposals. After that, it is for political representatives among themselves to ensure that appropriate channels are kept open to ensure real responses in the appropriate parliament to real concerns of citizens. In that way, even if the suigeneric union we have in Europe involves layered '*demoi*' of various kinds at various levels, there will still be real democracy in the conduct of our affairs, and real possibilities of citizen involvement.

Chapter 11

Do the 'regions' get a proper place in Europe?

Enlargement of the Union has brought in many small states as full members of the Union. Malta, Cyprus, Slovenia, Estonia, Latvia, Lithuania and the Slovak Republic all sit at the top table in Council as of right, and in aggregating states' votes for the purpose of ascertaining whether a majority of states is for a proposal each counts for one, as does Luxembourg among the founder Members. That is exactly how it should be in a confederal union of states. But there are certain curious comparisons. Major regions of large states, like the Veneto in Italy, or Bavaria in Germany, or Catalunya or the Basque Country in Spain, or Flanders or Wallonia in Belgium, or Scotland or Wales in the UK are the sites of strong feelings of national or regional identity. They are larger than or comparable in size and population with the smaller states I have listed above — and are indeed comparable in size also with Denmark, or Ireland, or Finland. Not surprisingly, many of them have strong political parties or movements seeking an enhanced degree of political and legislative autonomy, even to the point of a restored 'independence in Europe'. This is most marked in those whose citizens consider their so-called 'region' to be a historic nation within a larger state — sometimes a so-called 'stateless nation', though in fact all have substantial institutions of state albeit well short of independent statehood.

There is here a matter of interest and possible concern to European constitutional reformers. Some have suggested that alongside of states, there may need to be recognition of 'partner regions' with significantly state-like characteristics for the purposes of successfully democratic self-governance within the total ensemble of the European Union. Alain Lamassoure, French MEP, distinguished former minister and Conventioneer, took up this idea during 2001–2, and in his draft Report to the European Parliament on the division of competences of the European Union and Member States[1], he included a proposal about recognition of what he called 'partner regions' in Europe. This idea received some favourable attention, in Scotland and others of the regions I mentioned above, as well as yet others not mentioned. Other versions of essentially the same concept focussed on the concept of 'regions with legislative power', and outside the explicit constitutional framework of Europe a network of such regions has been operating for some time. However, by a compromise, this idea was dropped from Alain Lamassoure's Report, and a whole new report was prepared by the EP's Constitutional Affairs Committee with its president Giorgio Napolitano acting as rappporteur.

This advised a more uniform approach with all regions on a substantially equal footing regardless of history and constitutional character. Still, it acknowledged the need to take account of differentiation of functions, and especially to have regard for those regions whose parliaments are responsible for the legislative implementation of framework laws laid down by the Union, and having executive and administrative responsibility for seeing to the implementation of Union laws. The extended references to 'regional and local government' in the definition of subsidiarity and in the Protocol on Subsidiarity and Proportionality reflect something of these concerns. But of course many voices from the Member States and the Committee of the Regions and much evidence submitted to the Convention by many regional governments gave backing to the general idea, so no single source can claim sole credit for its adoption.

The role that fell to me in the Convention, as a European Free Alliance MEP, was that of the sole elected representative of a specifi-

---

[1]   See European Parliament resolution on the Communication from the Commission entitled 'Report on the division of competences between the European Union and the Member States, (2001/2024(INI))' (Lamassoure Report).

cally 'civic nationalist'[2] or 'regionalist' opinion at the Convention. There were other stout supporters of the regionalist version of this cause, among whom I remember most vividly Erwin Teufel, Minister President of Baden Würtemberg, a German Parliament representative at the Convention. Then there were also Mme Claude du Granrut from Picardy and Manfred Dammeyer from North Rhine Westphalia who took part as observers from the Committee of the Regions. Dany Pieters of the New Flemish Alliance was an alternate member representing the Belgian Parliament. Various others spoke up from time to time, including Commissioner Michel Barnier, whose Commission responsibilities embraced regional issues as well as constitutional ones. Peter Hain in his role as Secretary of State for Wales spoke trenchantly in the debate about regions on 7 February 2003, and my old friend Robert MacLennan (Lord MacLennan of Rogart) as an alternate from the UK Parliament offered another Scottish voice. He and I did some work together about subsidiarity, trying to strengthen the idea of the necessity of local discretion to apply local knowledge.

Our proposal was by way of strengthening the definition of subsidiarity. If the point of legislation at European level is to determine essential matters of principle, how do you draw the line against excessive detail? One possibility would be by way of a constitutional presumption in favour of a certain degree of local discretion. The text I drafted about this said:

> The authorities of the Member States responsible for implementing a Community measure shall be entitled to exercise a sufficient margin of appreciation in order to implement it in a way which takes due account of specific local circumstances. They shall act so as to secure that the stated reasons on which the measure is based are satisfied in accordance with the principle of proportionality in the light of prevailing local circumstances. This margin of appreciation applies except where a Community measure expressly excludes it, the exclusion being justified in the stated reasons for the measure.

I confess to being more disappointed than surprised that this did not gain acceptance. Subsequently, I pursued similar ideas in a different context through a Report to the European Parliament on 'Target-based tripartite contracts and agreements between the

---

[2] For my conception of 'civic nationalism', see *Questioning Sovereignty* (MacCormick, 1999), chapter 10.

commission, Member States and regional or local authorities'[3]. My original draft Report was somewhat watered down in the Constitutional Affairs Committee's vote of November 2003. But after some hard work, and by making some reasonable compromises with colleagues from other parties, I was delighted when the Parliament finally adopted the re-amended text that I proposed to the Plenary Session of December 2003. It now remains to be seen what, if anything, will come of this in the way of opening up general laws to the exercise of local knowledge and understanding. That is essentially up to the Commission working in dialogue with relevant levels of government in Member States.

Members of the Convention were able to submit written contributions. Together with colleagues in the European Free Alliance, through a series of meetings in the spring and early summer of 2002 in Strasbourg, Brussels, Berlin, Seville, Bilbao, Barcelona, and Brno, I produced a contribution to the Convention under the title 'Democracy at many levels: European Constitutional Reform'. This represented the position of the EFA fraction within our Parliamentary Group, but also took account of the wider concerns of EFA parties not represented in the European Parliament. It is interesting to look back on that and see how far matters turned out as we argued they should.

The basic theme was one of wholehearted support for the constitutional development of the European Union in a way that would be favourable for democracy and thus for the flourishing of all the peoples of Europe in a context of peace, security and sustainable all-round prosperity. The governing principle to which we appealed was that of self-determination for all the peoples of Europe. This, we pointed out, implies acknowledging the possibility of 'internal enlargement' of the Union. Just as new states can enter from outside, so two or more new states might emerge from within the Union in succession to an existing Member State. As a principle, self-determination can operate at more than one level in the construction of a new and better European Union. In Europe, it ought to include full recognition of the right to self-government of all those territorial entities in the Union whose citizens have a

---

[3]   See European Parliament resolution on the Communication from the Commission entitled 'A framework for target-based tripartite contracts and agreements between the Community, the States and regional and local authorities' (COM(2002) 709 - 2003/2088(INI)), (MacCormick Report)

strong and shared sense of national, linguistic, or regional identity, whether such entities are already recognised as states or as self-governing entities of one kind or another, or remain for the present unrecognised in the constitutional structure of state.

The Constitution, I must say, does not anywhere acknowledge the principle of self-determination in this sense. Indeed, in one respect it can be read as expressing hostility to it. The second sentence of Article I-5 (1), dealing with relations between the Union and the states says that '[The Union] shall respect their essential State functions, including ensuring the territorial integrity of the State, maintaining law and order and safeguarding national security.' This certainly could not be read, for example, as prohibiting the United Kingdom and Ireland from agreeing the transfer of present-day Northern Ireland into the Republic of Ireland, if the people of Northern Ireland voted in favour of this in a referendum. This possibility is indeed envisaged in the 'Good Friday' agreement of 1988 and the associated British and Irish legislation. Nor indeed could it be read as precluding the reunification of Gibraltar with Spain, if the people of Gibraltar were to ask for this, or consent to it. Many UK Prime Ministers have said that the United Kingdom was a union established by agreement between Scotland and England in the first instance, and subsequently between Great Britain and Ireland, of which only Northern Ireland now remains in that union. Hence if the settled will of the Scottish people ever became determined for dissolution of the Anglo-Scottish union, appropriate steps would be taken to secure the independence of Scotland and of the remaining kingdom, whether a Britain comprising England and Wales or, indeed, England and Wales as mutually independent entities.

The point of Article I-5, it seems to me, is to ensure that the EU may not in any way influence political developments to bring about such a conclusion. It must leave such an issue to the internal constitutional processes of the states that are currently the Member States of the Union. It says nothing, however, about how the Union is to respond if such developments do take place by popular decision within a member State or its internal regions or nations. Above all, the provision in question most naturally to concern the integrity of territory against external encroachments. Areas where this might be apprehended are certain border zones of new Member States in eastern and central Europe, where, for example, there are areas populated by ethnic Hungarians in Slovakia and Rumania, ethnic Slovaks in Hungary, and so on.

Indeed, the presupposition on which the Constitution rests is the sovereignty over their own internal constitution of the Member States who together sustain and empower the Union. The Union leaves all questions about governmental structures at this level exclusively to the States. As a confederalist myself, I cannot fairly object to this.

On the other hand, one may conversely welcome the opening sentence of Article I-5 (1) 'The Union shall respect the equality of Member States before the Constitution as well as their national identities, inherent in their fundamental structures, political and constitutional, inclusive of regional and local self-government.' I note also, according to Article I-58 (1) of the Draft,

> The Union shall be open to all European States which respect the values referred to in Article I-2, and are committed to promoting them together.
>
> 2. Any European State which wishes to become a member of the Union shall address its application to the Council.

This opens a door to internal enlargement, but Article 58(2) goes on to stipulate that a new State's acceptance into membership is dependent on unanimity in the European Council. The converse aspect of self-determination is to be found in the 'exit clause', Article I-60 on 'Voluntary Withdrawal from the Union', which can be achieved by 'any Member State which decides to withdraw.'

Apart from the claim of self-determination, we in EFA supported the idea that the Convention's essential task was to produce a Constitution for the European Union, taking the existing constitutional structure and transforming it into a formal constitution with adequate guarantees for democracy, subsidiarity, cultural and linguistic pluralism, human rights and the protection of minorities in the Union. The Charter of Fundamental Rights would be one corner-stone in this, and the establishment for the future of an acceptable process of constitutional reform replacing the present *ad hoc* approach another. I would unhesitatingly claim that the Convention rose well to this task that we considered essential. The Constitution text meets the desiderata we stated, especially in its incorporation of the Charter of Fundamental Rights as Part II of the Constitution.

The powers of the Union (exclusive, shared, or complementary powers), we said, need to be expressly stated, and perhaps put in somewhat clearer terms than in the Treaties as they stand now. The powers of the Member States and of the self-governing territorial entities within them had to be expressly acknowledged as covering everything not expressly transferred to the institutions of the Union. These demands were also well satisfied. The Constitution is indeed a clear and straightforward document in its essential Parts, I and II. Certainly, there is a lot of detail in Part III, but it has already been explained why this is necessary.

A critical question for EFA was whether the Council or the Commission should be the principal bearer of the executive power of the Union. For the Union to have a democratic character with fair participation by states and entities varied in size, we took it to be vital that the Commission bear this role, under the strategic guidance of the European Council and answerable to the European Parliament. In essence, despite the slightly tricky compromises involving the two Presidencies — of Commission and of Council — the Constitution squares also with this position of ours.

The Council of Ministers, we argued, ought to be redesigned somewhat to reveal its role as one of the two chambers of the legislature of Europe, that which represents the states and territories of the Union, and which reaches its decisions typically by qualified majority voting. The European Parliament, which is the other legislative Chamber, ought to have power of co-decision with the Council on all matters within the legislative competence of the Union. This we considered an essential step in building a fully democratic scheme of European self-government.

Here again, the Constitution matches up reasonably well to the proposals we put forward. The ordinary legislative process under it will have just this character, and will apply very generally, though not yet quite universally, in the Union's lawmaking activities. But the Council will not be open to the internal nations and territories of the States to the extent that we considered desirable. Still, it remains the case that 'the Council shall consist of a representative of each Member State at ministerial level who may commit the government of the Member State in question and cast its vote.' (Article I-23(2)) It is for the states, not the Union, to decide in accordance with their own constitutional arrangements which ministers from what levels of government may exercise this representative function. Belgium is regularly represented either by a Flemish or by a Walloon minister; Germany, on matters within *Land* competence by a regional minister appointed to the function by the *Bundesrat*; and the United Kingdom may be represented by a Scottish or Welsh Minister (possibly, in due course, by one from Northern Ireland). More usual, however, is the practice whereby the 'regional' minister participates in, but does not lead at Council, as representative of the UK. Spain, by contrast, has resisted all overtures aimed at enabling Catalunya or the Basque Country (Euskadi), or Galicia or indeed any autonomous region to take any part in the Council.

Subsidiarity, along with democracy and self-determination, was for us the major issue for the Convention. The Constitution had to give it a better and stronger definition, one that the Courts could elaborate as a constitutional principle in the light also of the decisions of political decision-makers. For countries or territorial entities like those represented by EFA in the 1999-2004 European Parliament (Andalucia, Catalunya, Euskadi, Flanders, Galicia, Scotland, and Wales) in their present constitutional situation, a satisfactory understanding of subsidiarity was essential. Appropriate recognition of their role as partners in the governance of the Union was a requirement of a satisfactory constitutional settlement. So important was this, that I subsequently submitted a separate Contribution on 'Subsidiarity, Common Sense, and Local Knowledge', and some amendments aimed at strengthening early drafts of the Constitution on this point.

A previous chapter indicates the progress that we made. Still, however, the Constitution locates the element of decentralised parliamentary control of these principles in the central parliaments of the Member States. It then leaves the further iteration of the principles to them: 'It will be for each national Parliament or each chamber of a national Parliament to consult, where appropriate, regional parliaments with legislative powers' (Subsidiarity Protocol, Article 6). It was a matter for regret that the Praesidium of the Convention did not accede to the many requests that it should establish a Working Group to examine the place of self-governing territorial entities ('regions') and local authorities in the European architecture and similar issues. One day of debate at the Convention was dedicated to this issue, but without the benefit of the kind of Working Group Report that was available for other important issues, and probably no more could have been achieved given the general composition of Convention and Praesidium.

Some other more detailed points merit mentioning. The European Free Alliance unsuccessfully urged the Convention to improve its terminology to avoid the inappropriate use of the term 'region' to refer to territorial entities within the Union, which their citizens regard as 'nations', and to avoid the ideological use of concepts like 'nation state', especially in contrast to 'region'. We proposed that there should be genuine reform of parliamentary representation in the European Parliament. This should secure that in all save quite small states there are electoral constituencies that recognise areas with a distinctive sense of national or regional identity, and that take particular account of existing territorial entities that have achieved constitutional recognition. This is already the case in the United Kingdom and in Belgium, and to a degree in Germany, but not, for example in Spain, with the result that Basque, Catalan and Galician (and other regionalist) parties have difficulty achieving anything like fairly proportional representation in the European Parliament. The Constitution takes no step forward in this, Article I-20 leaving it to the European Council in future on the initiative of the European Parliament and with its consent to adopt a decision allocating seats to states, on the principle of degressive proportionality, with a minimum number of six seats for any state, a maximum of ninety-six, and a total ceiling of seats set at 750. (Already, Malta has five to Wales's four, with Galicia even more thinly represented via all-Spain lists, not regional constituencies. In due course Malta will increase to six for its population of just under 400,000. This does not look like a good deal for large 'regions' or 'stateless nations' in large member states, larger German *Länder* being proportionately the worst off.

A similar lack of success attended our attempt to reform the Committee of Regions to make it more genuinely a regionally based body rather than a Committee to which the states in their discretion send regional and local government representatives. For this, similar degressive proportionality principles apply to those governing the European Parliament. The effect of this is that Malta and Luxembourg are more numerously represented on this Committee than Wales or Scotland, or, indeed London or Yorkshire. For the future, the states will remain very much in the driving seat: 'The number of members of the Committee of the Regions shall not exceed 350. The

Council, acting unanimously on a proposal from the Commission, shall adopt a European decision determining the Committee's composition' (Article III-386). Our view was that the Committee should be reformed or abolished, and the case for reform remains powerful.

On the other hand, as the Protocol on the Application of the Principles of Subsidiarity and Proportionality shows, our representations that regions with legislative powers must be consulted by the Commission in drafting legislation were substantially successful. Our wish to see stronger provisions concerning the rights of regions to be represented at the Council, with the possibility of splitting a member State's vote to reflect different regional opinions did not succeed. However, as noted earlier, the right to participation of regional ministers at the Council remains unimpaired, but is wholly dependent on each State's own constitutional arrangements in this regard. A further point put forward by EFA concerned access to the Court of Justice. We proposed opening access to all territorial entities exercising legislative and governmental powers within a state and under its constitution. These must be enabled to seek judicial review of Union legislation that invades their constitutional competences, with a view to ensuring due respect for the principle of subsidiarity in their case. As noted in the discussion of subsidiarity, it remains with Member State parliaments and the Committee of the Regions to take up complaints about subsidiarity with the Court. The general right of access to the Court for all natural and legal persons will, however, be somewhat extended, and this may create an opportunity for internal-territorial governments and parliaments to challenge Union legislation in certain very restricted cases. Under Article III-363 (4), 'Any natural or legal person may, under the conditions laid down in paragraphs 1 and 2, institute proceedings against an act addressed to that person or which is of direct and individual concern to him or her, and against a regulatory act which is of direct concern to him or her and does not entail implementing measures.' With regard to regulatory acts impinging on constitutional powers of regional authorities, it is possible that this will open the door to those regional authorities which constitute legal persons under the constitutional law of their own state.

We further argued that the Parliaments of self-governing entities in member-states should be better involved in the European institutional system. Those exercising legislative powers should be able to participate in the parliamentary trans-European network known as COSAC — Conférence des Organes Spécialisés dans les Affaires Communautaires (Conference of Community and European Affairs Committees). On this, no advance was achieved. The provisions concerning COSAC in the Draft Protocol on the Role of National Parliaments in the European Union relates solely to Parliaments at Member State level, and does not envisage any mechanism for involvement of other parliaments within the States. Networks of such parliaments with legislative powers are coming into existence by independent effort, without any constitutional recognition at Union level (except in so far as sub-sets of the Committee of the Regions are involved).

Finally, we demanded better recognition for the linguistic diversity of the European Union. All languages must be recognised as essential elements of the rich heritage of the EU, and all languages and cultures should have equal rights, as stated in the Universal Declaration of Linguistic Rights, signed in Barcelona in 1996. All official languages in the territory of the European Union must be given proper status at the European level. We therefore support the EBLUL (European Bureau for Lesser Used Languages) proposals to the Convention. On this, there was a real success. Article I-3 (3) fourth indent says: 'The Union shall respect its rich cultural *and linguistic* diversity, and shall ensure that Europe's cultural heritage is safeguarded' (italics added).

The Convention's Draft Constitution, all the more following the final amendments and adjustments at the Inter-Governmental Conference, represents a robustly statist, and to that extent, confederal, vision of the Union. It is a Union whose powers are conferred on it by the Member States that set it up. Their internal constitutional arrangements remain entirely their own affair. To the extent that these arrangements empower stateless nations or other territorial collectivities in the form of legislative or administrative regions, the Union's institutions are obliged to take account of these, and of local authorities as well. Linguistic and cultural diversity is more generously recognised than hitherto. Subsidiarity is better defined and will probably be better policed and observed. From the point of view of the European Free Alliance, I judge this to be worth two cheers, albeit not the full three. It is certainly better than anything achieved so far in this general direction, at all-Europe level.

Chapter 12

Fisheries —
a special problem

Finally, I turn to a very specific issue of what might be considered in several senses (as we shall see) a 'regional' issue that was and is of great concern to me. The fishing industry is a vital element in the economy of some of the most peripheral and fragile regions and islands within Scotland, thus some of the most peripheral and fragile and culturally distinctive parts of Europe. If Scottish — or Basque, or Galician, — fishing were to die or be extinguished by ill-judged policy emanating from the Union's law and institutions, this would bring grave discredit to the whole enterprise. Certainly, even those in Scotland who are most wedded to the idea of enhanced integration through a better constituted Union would give up on it in disgust. I am one of those. During the Convention process and in its aftermath I was sorely tested.

When considering the issue mentioned earlier about 'partner regions', it is easy to see how odd it is that a landlocked state like Luxembourg has greater influence on the Common Fisheries Policy (hereafter 'CFP') than Scotland can have. As more states that are either landlocked or remote from the North Atlantic and North Sea, or both, enter the Union, the problem grows worse. On one occasion, I reminded the Convention that the Slovak Republic and Scotland have more or less exactly the same population, but Slovakia has no coastline while Scotland's is very extensive and accounts for a very large proportion of the community fishing waters in the North Atlantic and North Sea. Yet Scotland has, as such, no vote at the Fisheries Council, while Slovakia will take a full part under whatever system of qualified majority voting is prevalent at a given time. The introduction of Regional Advisory Councils under the latest comprehensive CFP Regulation (2371/2002) is intended to improve the involvement of real stakeholders in the design and implementation of policies to secure a sustainable fishing industry. But it remains to be seen how effective this will be in giving an opportunity for a Scottish voice to be heard proportionately to the scale of Scotland's involvement. Being merely 'advisory' is not a way to inspire confidence.

When it came to the 'writing' phase of the Convention, among the earliest of the draft articles laid before Conventioneers were those that have become Articles I-13, and I-14. The former lists the areas in which the Union exercises 'exclusive competence', the latter, those where competence is shared between the Union and the Member States. Exclusive competence included, and in the final version of the text still includes, 'the conservation of marine biological resources under the common fisheries policy', the rest of the domains of the common fisheries policy being within shared competence under I-14. The fisheries conservation element sits a little oddly alongside of historically central and essential topics as the customs union, the competition rules essential to the internal market, monetary policy in respect of the euro, and the common commercial policy. (The Union also has exclusive competence in relation to concluding international agreements where this is expressly provided for in a legislative act of the Union, or insofar as its conclusion may affect common rules or alter their scope.')

The current Community Treaty makes but brief reference to fisheries at all. Article 3 (1) (e) commits the Community to having a 'common policy in the sphere of agriculture and fisheries'. Title II of Part 3 of the Treaty (Articles 32-38) is headed 'Agriculture', but Article 32(1) includes the remarkable provision that '"Agricultural products" means the products of the soil, of stockfarming and of fisheries'. It is assumed that whatever applies to agriculture applies to fisheries as well, regardless of any of the obvious differences between the two. One might as well say that herring and haddock can be deemed a kind of cabbage or cauliflower. Yet the whole law-making power in respect of fisheries grows out of this remarkable stipulative definition saying what the term 'agricultural products' is to be understood as meaning. It was on this basis that the regulation defining the CFP was adopted by the original six in 1970 the day after the negotiations for the entry of the UK, Ireland, Denmark and Norway had started. The Accession Treaty and Act of the

UK and of the other new member states of the first enlargement in 1973 (Norway having refused to join on the terms offered about fisheries) made extensive transitional and other provisions for adapting to the CFP. The transitional period came to an end on 31 January 1978.

Coastal states do retain certain rights in their inshore waters up to six miles, and, with further qualifications, in a further band of water six miles beyond that. This is a qualification that has been extended several times since first agreed on an in-principle temporary basis, and is not currently due to expire before 2012. By several judicial decisions, notably that by the European Court of Justice in litigation between the Commission and the United Kingdom in *Case 804/79*, it has long since been laid down that, since the end of the transitional period that concluded at the end of 1978, the whole power of regulating fisheries conservation in Community waters belongs to the Community Institutions. It is exercisable by the Council acting on proposals put forward by the Commission. Member States have no further regulatory power save such as might be expressly delegated back to them by the Community.

In this condition of things, two possible views might be taken about the provision of Article I-13 about fisheries conservation. On the one hand, it might be said, and was said, that this simply gave explicit constitutional recognition to what is implicit in the current Treaties, including treaties of accession. On the other, it could be argued that the express inclusion of this 'exclusive competence' in Part I of the treaty amounted to a further entrenchment of a case-law based legal regime that had grown steadily more contentious over the years. In early 2003 the main debates about exclusive competence took place at the Convention's plenary session of 27-28 February followed by a special working session chaired by Giuliano Amato on 5 March. At that time, the Common Fisheries Policy had come under more than usually fierce criticism in Scotland, in circumstances triggered by an apparent drastic diminution of breeding stocks of cod in the North Sea. The response of the EU, based on proposals of the Commission that were amended after the usual horse-trading at the Council of Ministers in December 2002, seemed to most participants from the Scottish side to be disproportionately unfavourable to the Scottish white fish fleet. Ross Finnie, the Scottish Minister for Fisheries, and Eliot Morley, his UK counterpart, who of course led for the UK at the Council, claimed they had obtained the best result available for Scotland, but other observers contended that they had been isolated and then outvoted on key points.

Whatever the truth of that matter may be, there was in the winter of 2003 a profound sense of crisis affecting the fishing industry, so vital as it is to many of the more peripheral parts of Scotland. The fishing industry in Scotland, of course, accounts for a much larger proportion of Scotland's GDP than does the UK industry as whole in relation to the United Kingdom's GDP. Moreover, by contrast with Norway and even more sharply with the Faeroes and Iceland, the European Union over the years since inauguration of the CFP has clearly failed to achieve a properly sustainable fisheries policy while observing a fair balance among the countries involved in fisheries. This applies also to the critically important downstream fish processing industries and other ancillary activities, such as boat building, chandlery and such like. The cod crisis of November/December 2002 and its aftermath seem clearly to show that the European Union's approach to conservation has not worked, by contrast with the relative success of small neighbouring states. The Commission and its allies claim that the fault for this lies partly with the Member States, for horse-trading at the Council rather than focussing on real conservation needs, and partly with the fishing industry itself, since its members fish in a long-run self-defeating way, cheating and landing more fish than their quotas allow.

What I have just written is based on reading and conversation with those more directly involved. In the Convention, by contrast, I gained direct evidence. Although the Government representative Peter Hain had been at an earlier stage critical of the listing of exclusive competences, he dropped this line of argument by the time the second last Draft was in circulation in May 2003, and I found myself unable successfully to establish contact with him in order to explain the seriousness of the situation. Gisela Stuart MP took note of my concerns, however, and advised me to address them to Henning Christoffersen, the Danish former Prime Minister, who was rightly considered the fisheries expert on the Praesidium. His advice to me was that since all that was in issue was resource conservation *under the CFP*, there was nothing to worry about — and, anyway, the fish in the North Sea do not observe national boundaries, hence must be protected by a common régime of conservation. When I said that I could not possibly convince my own constituency that there was nothing to worry about, and explained what my constituency was, he visibly lost interest in the argument. Denmark, of course, as a Member State with five million citizens has noticeably succeeded better than similarly-sized Scotland in sustaining its fishing industry within the confines of the CFP.

Colleagues in the Westminster Parliament subsequently took the matter up with Jack Straw, the Foreign Secretary, in the hope of activating the Government during the IGC. His reply, however, was that the references to the CFP in the Constitution were an accurate reflection of the current legal position. Hence he considered it inappropriate to challenge them at the stage of finalising the Constitution text.

In effect, nobody aware of the issue at the Convention was sufficiently interested in securing SNP support for ratification of the constitution-treaty to take the trouble to argue for a fresh look at the 'exclusive competence' issue. This no doubt seemed reasonable enough at a time at which the UK government's doctrine was that ratification would be a matter for parliamentary decision without any need for a referendum. Then suddenly, in the run-up to the European Parliamentary Election of June 2004, the Prime Minister (apparently without even informing, far less consulting, the Cabinet) performed a U-turn. He declared that there would, after all, be a referendum to decide whether or not the UK should ratify the treaty establishing the constitution. This made alienation of the SNP highly risky given the knife-edge outcome that already seemed the best the government could hope for in the referendum to which it had so casually been committed.

Until close to the end of the IGC process, an air of indifference continued to prevail. Despite pressure by SNP Members in the Scottish Parliament and in the Westminster Parliament, the Government discovered no 'red line' affecting the CFP, by contrast with other important issues such as energy. (In that case, Part III of the Convention-approved text had made what appeared to be alarming innovations, but these were cut out and dropped in good time.) A body of potential support was being neglected, for at its Annual Conference in 2003, the SNP had declared itself cordially in favour of the constitution proposed by the Convention, but unable to accept it or support ratifying it unless there were a change on the exclusive competence concerning conservation of marine biological resources.

Was this a reasonable point of view? Once it is conceded that the constitution reproduces the effect of existing case law interpreting the present treaties and regulations made under them, someone might ask what is so upsetting to the SNP? The answer lies, obviously enough, in the character of a constitution. Whatever is expressly laid down in a constitution can only be altered by a constitutional amendment. Where a constitution is enshrined in a treaty, there has to be a determination of an amendment process that takes account of the way in which the Constitution is encapsulated in a Treaty. The Constitution, broadly in line with the original Convention draft, proposes that for any future changes of substance, amendments would be required through a fresh convention-cum-IGC process. In these circumstances, any hope of getting the exclusive competence clause and the underlying case-law revisited and amended looks pretty dim.

Not everything is set in stone, of course. At issue is 'conservation … under the CFP.' But the CFP in turn is defined by a Regulation (what will in future be called a 'European law'). That Regulation or Law is itself subject to alteration by the appropriate legislative process. At present, this is in the power of the Council only, with consultation of the Parliament. If the Constitution does come into force, the CFP Regulation will become subject to the ordinary legislative process, with Parliament playing a fully co-ordinate role with the Council of Ministers in law-making. There will be no requirement of unanimity, that is, no constitutional entrenchment of the CFP in any of those aspects that currently depend on ordinary legislation (so-called 'secondary Community law'). As the Royal Society of Edinburgh observes (RSE 2003), however, the principle of subsidiarity applies only to matters that fall within shared competence. If resource conservation is a matter of exclusive competence, the Union authorities are entitled if they see fit to delegate powers back to the States, but they are under no obligation to restrict their legislative effort to those matters which can be dealt with effectively only at all-Union level.

What Mr Christoffersen said to me is true enough. Conserving the resources of the sea cannot be done on strictly national lines, given the mobility and in some cases the migratory quality of fish. Does it follow that it must be an all-Union deliberation? Must Swedes and Danes and Finns debate about the Mediterranean? Or Maltese and Italians and Slovenians and Cypriots the North Atlan-

tic or the Baltic? Do land-locked states have ministerial or other
expertise to contribute relevantly to issues concerning sea fisheries
anywhere? In a union of twenty-five, the existing style of legislative
authority over the fisheries policy will become an absurdity.

It was on these grounds that I lodged, and again re-lodged, an
amendment to Article I-12, advocating the removal of reference to
fisheries from exclusive competences. The gist of the argument I put
before the Convention about this was that there was (and continues
to be) a strong current of opinion in favour of a much greater decen-
tralisation of the governance of fisheries and marine resources.
Whether this view will prevail or not, it would be totally unacceptable to entrench an exclusive competence that could in turn be
changed only by a Constitutional amendment, with the risk of
obstructing a reasonable move towards taking a more seriously
regional view of fisheries problems.

A different way of getting at substantially the same question was
through Part III of the Constitution. There, the existing treaties are
revised and put into order with respect to Part I. As I have mentioned, the existing Community Treaty, like all its predecessors,
handles fisheries as an apparent afterthought. To discover what
there is in the way of fisheries policy, one must turn to the section
labelled 'Agriculture'. There, no more is to be found than that whatever is said about agriculture and agricultural policy or agricultural
products shall be deemed to apply also to fisheries. On so flimsy a
foundation was the Common Fisheries Policy erected, a hasty
addendum to the Common Agricultural Policy developed just in
time to forestall full involvement in its design by the UK, Denmark
Ireland and Norway.

The production of Part III was treated by the Convention as pri-
marily a technical exercise. The legal experts of the Council, the
Commission and the Parliament took on the task of re-casting additional treaty law in the required way, indicating the changes they
saw as required. They flagged up for attention only those that
seemed to require some political choice guided by the established
consensus of the Convention. In relation to the section that concerns
me, all they had done was to add 'and fisheries' to the Chapter heading. Then they made a minor amendment to the introductory article
to express the fact that an Agriculture and Fisheries Policy was cov-
ered by this Chapter. (Incidentally, this itself is misleading; there is

still no 'agriculture and fisheries policy'. There is an agriculture policy and also a quite distinct fisheries policy).

Fortunately, it was possible for Conventioneers to propose amendments even to this allegedly technical part of the Constitution. I did so, on the ground that this was no time to be transposing an already unsatisfactory part of the previous treaties into the new Constitution with all the same absurdities.

This campaign of amendment aimed to ensure that fisheries were recognised as different in some important characteristics from agriculture. The first version of the attack suggested dropping the definition of 'agricultural products' as including 'products ... of fisheries', and inserting a new provision about fisheries in the following terms:

> The provisions of the Constitution shall apply to the products of the fishing industry and of the first-stage processing thereof as though these were agricultural products, but only so far as is consistent with the specific characteristics of the fishing industry. Subject to the same qualification, references to the common agricultural policy and the use of the term 'agricultural' shall apply to fisheries.
>   The fishing industry, by contrast with agriculture, exists only in certain Member States, and in these it is strongly regional in its economic and social relevance. It is also regional in the sense of involving regional groups of Member States having geographical propinquity to or historical associations with particular fishing zones and fisheries. These facts partly determine the specific character of this industry and must be fully taken into account.

This was a good try albeit rather prolix. It produced a certain effect. At the instance of the Praesidium or the secretariat (or both, for all I know) the offending text was revised a little, though not as extensively as I had proposed. Under the heading 'Agriculture and Fisheries', what is now Article III-225 qualifies what is said about fisheries with the words 'having regard to the specific characteristics of this sector.' Here is the whole thing:

> The Union shall define and implement a common agriculture and fisheries policy.

> 'Agricultural products' means the products of the soil, of stockfarming and of fisheries and products of first-stage processing directly related to these products. References to the common agricultural policy or to agriculture, and the use of the term 'agricultural', shall be understood as also referring to fisheries, having regard to the specific characteristics of this sector.

Although I continued to press for the recognition of the doubly 're-gional' character of the fishing industry (and indeed of the conservation problem as well) I made no further progress. The task of the Convention was to produce a Constitution that would be intelligible to the citizens. So far as concerns one area of economic and social life of the Union, fisheries and fishing communities, the Convention fell short of addressing its audience convincingly. The treaty still says that '"Agricultural products" means the products of the soil, of stockfarming and of fisheries', welcoming us to a world in which haddocks and herrings are essentially in the same class as cabbages and cauliflowers. Given the differences (and lack of isomorphy) between agriculture and fisheries, there ought by now to have been recognition of two separate entities, a Common Agricultural Policy (CAP) and a Common Fisheries Policy (CFP).

Making a new Constitution could have provided an opportunity to abandon the confusion sown by the old order. At least the Union could have adopted an explicit provision that would permit the development of a new fisheries policy *sui generis*. It could have acknowledged the strongly regional quality of fish stocks and the fishing communities that make their living from them, and supply the citizens of the Union with this essential and healthy food source. Being thankful for small mercies, however, we see fisheries now recognised as a sector having quite specific characteristics of its own, albeit the Constitution is silent about what these are, and about which of the agricultural provisions therefore do not apply to it. Nothing explicit is said about the idea that this must imperatively come under a much more robust system of regional management, rather than being forever centralised in Brussels and dominated by decisions of a Council most of whose members have neither interest in nor available expertise concerning fisheries. I do note, however, that the incoming Fisheries Commissioner Joe Borg, former Foreign Minister of Malta, has spoken strongly in favour of developing the role of Regional Advisory Councils, and shows an apparently genuine sensitivity to the problems faced by fishing communities.

There is a final positive element to report. Although the United Kingdom government did not at any time think it worth pursuing any points about fisheries, the Irish Government, through its Minister for European Affairs, Mr Dick Roche, showed greater concern. In the latest phases of discussion of final adjustments to the Constitution prior to the concluding meeting of the IGC, Dick Roche received a group of SNP Members of the United Kingdom, the Scottish, and the European Parliaments in Strasbourg in April 2004 and took a real interest in the problem. For he saw clearly enough the difficulty about securing Scottish support for a Constitution that entrenched an unsatisfactory element of exclusiveness about fisheries in the context of relatively marginal improvement of the relevant Part III text.

Not until October, with publication of the definitive text did I discover that in an indirect way the final text of the Constitution contains a device that can potentially defuse this 'entrenchment' issue. Article IV-445 creates a new procedure for possible amendment of anything in Part III that deals with the internal policies of the Union ('Title III of Part III'). The European Council, acting by unanimity, may adopt a European decision amending all or part of the provisions of Title III, which of course includes Agriculture and Fisheries, among much else. The Council must consult the European Parliament and the Commission, and the decision may come into force only if it is approved by the Member States in accordance with their respective constitutional requirements. Such a decision may diminish, but may not increase, the competences accorded to the Union.

This cannot be said to amount to an easy process of amendment, but it is easier than anything that will be available if the Constitution is not adopted. It is already possible for the CFP Regulation to be amended by fresh legislation, and if the Constitution comes into force, this will be a matter for the ordinary legislative process. We recall that exclusive competence attaches to 'the conservation of marine biological resources *under the common fisheries policy.*' (italics added). If reforms in this do not prove satisfactory, the competences of the Union concerning fisheries are capable of being reduced or removed by the procedure laid down in III-445. This will never be easy, I repeat, but it would be easier than changing what currently exists if the Constitution is not adopted.

It would be good if the fishing states including, if not led by, the UK would set their minds to working towards radical reform so as to decentralise effectively the management of fish stocks and fisheries to the main fishing zones of the Union. They could insist that management bodies and fishing opportunities be structured so as to respect the fundamental principle of relative stability, securing to fishing communities a steady share of whatever sustainable fishing opportunities there are in a given fishery, and a commensurate share in management bodies. This, of course, can and must be done in a way that respects also the principle of non-discrimination on grounds of nationality. The Commission could carry this forward by introducing appropriate legislation, much less half-hearted than current 'regional advisory' provisions. By some such means Scotland and similar 'regions' or countries could reasonably and properly acquire a much more substantial role in the governance of northern fisheries than, for example, the Slovak Republic or Slovenia, which would have (and I suppose, would wish) none at all. Similar provisions could apply to the other large fishing regions of the Union.

It now appears to me that there is a slightly better chance for far-reaching reform of the CFP if the Constitution is adopted than if it is rejected. In an earlier incarnation, as the Scottish National Party's spokesperson on European Union affairs, I argued the case for supporting the Constitution as a welcome step towards democratising the Union, but not if the entrenchment of 'exclusive competence' in relation to fisheries conservation was retained. It now seems to me that, even on this deeply troublesome point, the balance of advantage is for the Constitution to be adopted rather than the old Treaties sustained in their latest (post-Nice) form. That is on top of the fact that for all the other reasons canvassed in the other chapters, the Constitution represents a large step forward in the enhanced democratisation of the Union.

Any state's membership of the European Union entails acknowledgement of the primacy of Union law on matters on which legislative competence has been conferred on the Union. In terms of traditional conceptions of sovereignty, this involves a voluntary derogation from full state sovereignty. It does not, however, entail transforming the Union into a sovereign entity in its own right. Moreover, each state retains the right to withdraw from the Union, thereby recovering its full sovereignty. This has, for most states involved, always been true as a matter of domestic law, but hitherto it was a doubtful point from the standpoint of Union law. If the Constitution is adopted, Article I-60 puts it beyond doubt that the right of exit belongs to each state if it chooses to exercise it in accordance with its own constitution. This will declare itself a voluntary Union, and the better for that.

Not every aspect of Union policy is satisfactory from every point of view. The Union has had failures as well as successes. But the balance of good over bad is very substantially in favour of the good. This will be more, not less, true, if the Union acquires a clearer, more intelligible and more democratic constitution. The existence of a peaceful and united — but not unitary — Europe makes the world a better place. That is what makes it right to support ratification of the Treaty establishing a Constitution for Europe.

References

For general reading on the European Constitutional Convention and on the emergence of the Constitution, see:

Norman, Peter (2003), *The Accidental Constitution* (Brussels: EuroComment)
Lamassoure, Alain (2004), *Histoire Secrète de la Convention européenne* (Paris: Fondation Robert Schumann/ Albin Michel)

Works referred to in the present text

Allott, Philip (2002), *The Health of Nations*. Cambridge: Cambridge University Press.
Booker, Christopher and North, Richard (2003), *The Great Deception: the Secret History of the European Union*. London: Continuum.
Dicey, A.V. (1961), *An Introduction to the Study of the Law of the Constitution*, 10th edn., ed E.C.S. Wade. London: Macmillan and Co.
Douglas-Scott, Seonaidh (2002), *Constitutional Law of the European Union*. London: Longman.
Grimm, Dieter (1995), 'Does Europe Need a Constitution?' I *European Law Journal*, 1.
Habermas, Jürgen (1992), 'Citizenship and National Identity: Some Reflections on the Future of Europe' 12 *Praxis International* 1.
MacCormick, Neil (1999), *Questioning Sovereignty: Law, State and Nation in the European Union*. Oxford: Oxford University Press.
Stuart, Gisela, MP (2003), *The Making of Europe's Constitution*. London: The Fabian Society.
Siedentop Larry (2000), *Democracy in Europe*. Harmondsworth, Middlesex: Allen Lane, The Penguin Press.
Weiler, J.H.H. (1999), *The Constitution of Europe*. Cambridge: Cambridge University Press.

SOCIETAS: essays in political and cultural criticism

Public debate has been impoverished by two competing trends. On the one hand the trivialization of the media means that in-depth commentary has given way to the soundbite. On the other hand the explosion of knowledge has increased specialization, and academic discourse is no longer comprehensible. As a result writing on politics and culture is either superficial or baffling.

This was not always so — especially for politics. The high point of the English political pamphlet was the seventeenth century, when a number of small printer-publishers responded to the political ferment of the age with an outpouring of widely-accessible pamphlets and tracts. Indeed Imprint Academic publishes facsimile C17th. reprints under the banner 'The Rota'.

In recent years the tradition of the political pamphlet has declined—with most publishers rejecting anything under 100,000 words. The result is that many a good idea ends up drowning in a sea of verbosity. However the digital press makes it possible to re-create a more exciting age of publishing. *Societas* authors are all experts in their own field, but the essays are for a general audience. Each book can be read in an evening. The books are available retail at the price of £8.95/$17.90 each, or on bi-monthly subscription for only £5/$10. Details: **imprint-academic.com/societas**

EDITORIAL ADVISORY BOARD

IMPRINT ACADEMIC, PO Box 200, Exeter, EX5 5YX, UK
Tel: (0)1392 841600   Fax: (0)1392 841478   sandra@imprint.co.uk
imprint-academic.com/societas

SOCIETAS

essays in political and cultural criticism

The Case Against the Democratic State
Gordon Graham

We are now so used to the state's pre-eminence in all things that few think to question it. This essay contends that the gross imbalance of power in the modern state is in need of justification, and that democracy simply masks this need with an illusion of popular sovereignty. Although the arguments are accessible to all, it is written within the European philosophical tradition. The author is Professor of Moral Philosophy at the Uniiversity of Aberdeen. 96 p., £8.95/$17.90

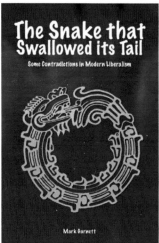

The Snake that Swallowed its Tail
Mark Garnett

Liberal values are the hallmark of a civilised society. Yet they depend on an optimistic view of the human condition, Stripped of this essential ingredient, liberalism has become a hollowed-out abstraction. Tracing its effects through the media, politics and the public services, the author argues that hollowed-out liberalism has helped to produce our present discontent. Unless we stop boasting about our values and try to recover their essence, liberal society will be crushed in the coils of its own contradictions. 96 pp., £8.95/$17.90

The Party's Over
Keith Sutherland

The book argues that the tyranny of the modern political party should be replaced by a mixed constitution in which advocacy is entrusted to an aristocracy of merit, and democratic representation is achieved via a jury-style lottery. 200 pp., £8.95/$17.90

• *'An extremely valuable contribution–a subversive and necessary read.'* **Graham Allen MP**, *Tribune*

• *'His analysis of what is wrong is superb . . . No one can read this book without realising that something radical, even revolutionary must be done.'* **Sir Richard Body**, *Salisbury Review*

• *'A political essay in the best tradition: shrewd, erudite, polemical, partisan, mischievous and highly topical.'* *Contemporary Political Theory*

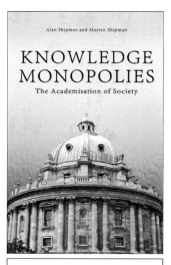

Knowledge Monopolies

Alan Shipman and Marten Shipman

Historians and sociologists chart the *consequences* of the expansion of knowledge; philosophers of science examine the *causes*. This book bridges the gap. The focus is on the paradox whereby, as the general public becomes better educated to live and work with knowledge, the 'academy' increases its intellectual distance, so that the nature of reality becomes more rather than less obscure.

96 pp., £8.95/$17.90

The Referendum Roundabout

Kieron O'Hara

A lively and sharp critique of the role of the referendum in modern British politics. The 1975 vote on Europe is the lens to focus the subject, and the upcoming referendum on the European constitution is also clearly in the author's sights.

Kieron O'Hara is author of *Trust: From Socrates to Spin* (2004) and *After Blair: Conservatism Beyond Thatcher* (2005) and *Plato and the Internet* (2002).

96 pp., £8.95/$17.90

Doing Less With Less
Making Britain More Secure
Paul Robinson

Don't believe neoconservative rhetoric on the 'war on terror': the twenty first century will be much safer. Armed forces designed for the cold war (and only maintained by vested interests within the defence bureaucracy) encourage global interference through pre-emption and other forms of military interventionism. We would be safer with less.

Paul Robinson has served as an army officer and is currently assistant director of the Centre for Security Studies at the University of Hull. His books include *The Just War in Comparative Perspective* (2003).

96 pp., £8.95/$17.90

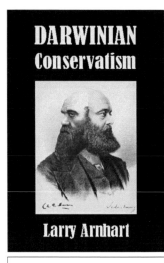

Darwinian Conservatism
Larry Arnhart

Darwinian biology sustains conservative social thought by showing how the human capacity for spontaneous order arises from social instincts and a moral sense shaped by natural selection in human evolution.

Larry Arnhart is a professor of political science at Northern Illinois University. He is the author of *Aristotle on Political Reasoning*, *Political Questions: Political Philosophy from Plato to Rawls*, and *Darwinian Natural Right: The Biological Ethics of Human Nature*.

96 pp., £8.95/$17.90

The Great Abdication
Alexander Deane

Our middle class has abstained from its responsibility to uphold societal values, and the enormously damaging collapse of our society's norms and standards is largely a result of that abdication. The institutions of political and social governance provide a husk of functionality and mask these problems for those that do not wish to see, or do not care. To restore Britain to something resembling a substantively functioning country, the middle classes must reinstate themselves as arbiters of morality, be unafraid to judge their fellow men, and follow through with the condemnation that necessarily follows when individuals sin against common values.

96 pp., £8.95/$17.90

The Moral Mind
Henry Haslam

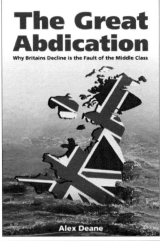

Haslam shows how important the moral sense is to the human personality and exposes the weakness in much current thinking that suggests otherwise. His goal is to help the reader to a mature and confident understanding of the moral mind, which constitutes an essential part of what it is to be human. The author writes from from a Judaeo-Christian background and addresses both believers and non-believers.

96 pp., £8.95/$17.90